A SPOTLIGHT ON THE METAPHYSICAL

EXPLORING EVERYTHING FROM CLARITY TO CRYSTALS

ANGIE TUTTERRO vv

Clarity and Crystals LLC
Copyright 2025, All rights reserved.
ISBN: 979-8-9988369-0-9 (paperback)
ISBN: 979-8-9988369-1-6 (e-book)

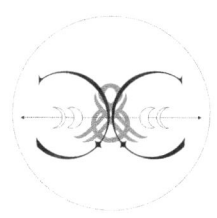

To the Gkids

Thank you for allowing me to leave you a legacy of words and magick.
The Spotlight will guide you on your journey if you choose to follow it.
You are strong.
You are powerful.
You can trust your own intuition.
I am always here if you need a guide along your path.
Be bold.
Take up space.
Love yourself the way I love you…
Fully, Fiercely, and without Apology.

~ Gigi

My intention for this book is simple

I want it to feel like we're sitting across from each other in a cozy coffee shop, each with a steaming cup of our favorite drink, just talking. Picture it, two friends catching up, sharing stories, and exchanging ideas without judgment or pretense. That's how I want this book to feel, like a conversation with someone you trust completely, where nothing is off-limits.

This is my story, my journey, and my way of sharing the things that have helped me along the way. Take what resonates with you, leave what doesn't, this isn't about rules or absolutes. It's about exploring, discovering, and finding what feels right for you.

Each chapter is designed to guide you through a different piece of this journey. It starts with Whispered Words, a gentle reflection to set the tone. Then we dive into the topic itself, exploring its depth and significance. Finally, you'll find Mentors, Guides, and Experts, a spotlight on the incredible people who have inspired and guided me.

So, go ahead, pour yourself that cup of coffee, tea, or whatever makes you feel most at home. Get comfortable, and let's chat. I can't wait to share this journey with you.

If you're craving more tools, stories, or just want to poke around in some metaphysical magick, come hang out with me at clarityandcrystals.com. It's where this book spills over into everyday life.

~ Angie

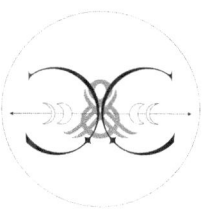

INTRODUCTION

Whispered Words

It wasn't until she was asked a simple, piercing question…
What is it you truly believe?
Is that what you really think, deep down in your soul?
Those words created space. A breath, a pause, a moment where questions rushed in like a tsunami, crashing against the edges of everything she thought she knew.
What is it I truly believe?
Who am I, really?
What am I doing with my life?
Why do I hold these beliefs?
Is this my truth?
Is this my inner knowing?
Is this the life I want to live?
Slowly, quietly, the answers began to surface. Like molten lava bubbling up from the depths of her soul, they couldn't be contained. They burst forth, raw and undeniable, shattering the silence she had held within for so long.
She searched.
She listened.
She sat still.
And one by one, thoughts began to form. Like pages in a book, her new story started to come together, lines she would write for herself, a life of her own choosing.
This was her truth.
Her knowing.
Her beliefs.
At the root of it all, she found herself.
This is who I am.
This is what I want.
This is what I believe and know.
These are my words. My truth. My life.

What This Book Is and What It's Not

Let's start by clearing up what this book is not. It's not a deep dive into every facet of the metaphysical and spiritual world. You won't find dense, overwhelming details or instructions here. Instead, this is a guide, a gentle introduction to the practices, ideas, and tools that have shaped my journey. This book is the kind of resource I wish I'd had when I started asking the big questions, the kind of guidance you'd hope to get from a trusted friend. It's not about giving you answers but pointing you toward your own truths.

More than anything, this book is a blueprint for myself. Putting these words on paper has helped me untangle my own thoughts, feelings, and beliefs. It's my way of understanding who I am, what I truly believe, and how I've arrived at this point in my life. It's my story, but it's also yours. My hope is that by sharing my journey and the tools I've used, you'll feel inspired to explore your own.

This journey began with questions, questions that gnawed at the edges of my mind, whispering for attention. Do I really believe the way I was raised? Is there more for me in this world? What do I truly want from my life? Is this all there is? These questions opened a doorway, one I couldn't close, and they led me to the path I'm on now.

Let me be clear: this is just a snapshot of where I am today. Beliefs evolve, ideas shift, and I'm still growing and learning every day. By the time I finish writing this book, I may already feel differently about parts of my journey. But the tools and practices that got me here, those are timeless. They've carried me this far, and I know they'll continue to guide me.

At my core, I see myself as a spotlight, someone who shares the knowledge and wisdom of others. This book is no different, it shines a light on the practices and people who have shaped me, offering them to you as you explore your own path. So, let's dive in.

My Journey

Writing this chapter feels like the hardest part of the book. Not because I don't know my story, but because putting it into words, sharing it with the world, makes it real. As I sit here in a quiet hotel room, trying to organize my thoughts, I realize why this is so difficult. I'm literally telling you that I don't know where to start, and that's exactly where I've been stuck: at the beginning.

Words are wands. They hold power. The words we speak shape our existence. They create our reality. And as I write this, I'm reminded that the story I'm telling is my truth. It's how I've spoken myself into being. So, here's my story, as honestly and simply as I can tell it.

I grew up in a conservative Christian household. Church wasn't just a part of our lives, it was the foundation of everything we did. If the church doors were open, we were there. My mom often worked as the church secretary, and my dad was deeply involved as a deacon or in other roles. My entire worldview was shaped through the lens of Christianity. I wasn't taught to question things; instead, everything was measured against the Bible. If it aligned, it was good. If it didn't, it was evil. That was the black-and-white world I lived in.

At 18, I chose to get married instead of going to college. At the time, I thought I was madly in love, and more than anything, I wanted to escape the confines of my upbringing. My parents didn't believe in dating, only courtship with the intention of marriage, so when I moved in with my boyfriend, I was essentially choosing my own path. Within two months, we were married.

Fast forward 22 years, three children, and a divorce later, I found myself at a crossroads. By then, I had already started questioning everything, who I was, what I believed, and what I wanted from life. For years, I had been living in a narrow, sheltered world, raising my children as I had been raised, without truly questioning if it was what I believed deep down.

But as they say, when the student is ready, the teacher appears. I met someone who challenged me to look at life differently, to question what I thought I knew. Those questions that had been quietly festering inside of me finally demanded answers:

Who am I?
What do I really want from my life?
Is this my truth, or someone else's?
Do I love myself?

Those questions opened the door to something greater. My journey into spirituality, my relationship with God, the Universe, and Source (GUS), began with baby steps. It wasn't about abandoning my past but about asking what I truly believed for myself. It was about rediscovering my soul and stepping into a life that felt like mine.

And here I am, still on that journey, still exploring, still asking the questions. This book is a snapshot of where I am today, a collection of the practices, tools, and insights that have helped me find clarity, heal, and grow. I hope it serves as a guide for you, just as these questions and tools have been for me.

Mentors, Guides, and Experts

Kathrin Zenkina - Manifestation Babe

Kathrin Zenkina, the creator of Manifestation Babe, has been a guiding light in understanding the power of manifestation and the law of attraction. Through her courses, books, and podcasts, she simplifies the art of manifesting, blending spirituality with actionable strategies that make transformation feel possible. Her teachings helped me reimagine my potential and truly believe in my ability to co-create with the universe.

manifestationbabe.com

Brandon Lucero - The New Generation Entrepreneur

Brandon Lucero, creator of The New Generation Entrepreneur, has transformed how I approach communication and entrepreneurship. Through his podcast and programs, he teaches how to craft messaging that connects on a deeper level and stands out with purpose. His guidance has helped me clarify my message and confidently share my ideas, making his work invaluable for anyone ready to elevate their voice and impact.

brandonlucero.com

Elizabeth Ralph - The Spiritual Investor

Elizabeth Ralph, founder of The Spiritual Investor, seamlessly blends spirituality with financial strategy, guiding individuals toward financial freedom through non-traditional methods. Her teachings have empowered me to view wealth creation as an energetic alignment, transforming my relationship with money into one of abundance and purpose.

thespiritualinvestor.com

NOTES

CLARITY

Whispered Words

Let's go back, back to life before she set it all aflame. Before the moments that forced her to choose. Before the decisions that unraveled the threads of her "supposed to be." Before she even knew she could question anything at all.

Back then, the mornings came early, often before the kids stirred. She would sit in the silence of a house not yet awake, savoring those fleeting moments before everything demanded her attention. Before the "Hey Mom!" started ringing out.

Morning routines had always been important, though she didn't fully understand why. She called it her time, a time to be the person she thought she was "supposed" to be. Quiet Time, she called it, beginning her day in the word and prayer, because that's what good mothers and good wives did. That's what she was told. That's what she believed.
The words she gave to those moments, Quiet Time, devotion, prayer, they didn't matter as much as the intention. Or maybe it was the illusion of intention.

The alarm went off. She rolled out of bed, mechanical in her movements, making sure he was awake and getting ready for work. Stumbling into the kitchen, she prepared his lunch, maybe started his truck if the weather was bad. She was the good wife, after all. She took care of the home and the family. That's what mattered.

She never stopped to wonder if this was what she wanted.
She didn't question.
She didn't dare.

Why would she? It was what she'd read in books, what she'd been taught in church, what she'd seen modeled by generations before her. The good wife. The good mother. The keeper of the family, the bearer of duty.

When he left for work, she'd pour herself a cup of coffee, settle into her favorite chair, Bible and notebook balanced on her lap. She spoke to God through the lens of her upbringing, recited her prayers, wrote in her journal. She checked the boxes dutifully.

Each tick of the checklist gave her a sense of validation. A hollow assurance that she was doing it right. That she was good. But good at what? At being someone else's idea of enough?

The days passed in routines, habits, and endless checklists. Rinse and repeat. Never questioning. Just doing. Just existing.

From the outside, it all looked perfect, the model family, the model life. But perfection is a fragile thing. A house of cards doesn't crumble from the top; it collapses from within. And if you looked too closely, if you asked too many questions, you'd see the cracks in the foundation.

But wasn't that exactly what she yearned for, deep down? For it all to fall apart? For the carefully constructed facade to shatter so she could finally see what was real?

She didn't know it then, but clarity was waiting for her, not in the perfect routine or the spotless house, but in the ashes of everything she thought she needed to be. Clarity wasn't about being good. It was about being whole. About burning it all down to find the truth buried beneath.

Habits as a Pathway to Clarity

Before we dive into clarity, let's talk about habits. Habits are the foundation, the cornerstone, the backbone of our daily lives. They shape everything we do, whether we realize it or not. Good or bad, conscious or unconscious, habits are the invisible threads that weave through our existence, creating the fabric of our days.

So, what is a habit? According to Webster, a habit is "a behavior pattern acquired by frequent repetition or physiological exposure that shows itself in regularity or increased facility of performance." My definition is a little simpler: a habit is something you do so consistently that it becomes second nature. It's the autopilot of life.

Think about your day. What are the things you do without even thinking? Brushing your teeth before bed? Reaching for coffee first thing in the morning? These are habits. But so are the little things you might not notice, like biting your nails when you're stressed or scrolling on your phone before you fall asleep. Habits are powerful. They can support us, or they can sabotage us. And here's the thing: I'm not here to tell you which habits are good or bad for you. I'm here to challenge you to think about how habits can work for you.

Have you ever heard of habit stacking? I first learned about it from James Clear's book, Atomic Habits. The concept is simple but brilliant: you take something you already do every day and stack a new habit on top of it. For example, let's say you want to start taking vitamins every night. If you already have the habit of brushing your teeth before bed, place your vitamins near your toothbrush. That way, every time you brush your teeth, you're reminded to take your vitamins. Before long, the two actions become one seamless routine.

Habit stacking has been a game-changer for me. It's how I've woven new practices into my life without feeling overwhelmed. Want to drink more water in the morning? Set a glass or bottle beside your coffee pot the night before. Want to start journaling? Keep a notebook on your nightstand and write down one thought before bed. It's not about overhauling your entire routine all at once, it's about integrating small, intentional changes that eventually become second nature.

Why am I dedicating a chapter to habits in a book about metaphysical practices? Because habits are the foundation of everything I do. For me, habits have always been a positive force. I've long been drawn to creating routines that support my health and well-being. At one point, I was making my own bread and even experimenting with homemade soap.

So, when I began exploring spiritual practices, it felt natural to integrate them into my existing routines through habit stacking.

This approach became the cornerstone of my metaphysical journey. It's how I created space for practices like meditation, journaling, and tuning into the moon's energy. By stacking these spiritual habits onto my daily routines, I transformed the mundane into something magickal. For example, I started journaling by stacking it with my morning coffee. While the coffee brewed, I'd write down my thoughts or set an intention for the day. I began meditating at night by stacking it with my bedtime routine, turning off the lights and focusing on my breath for just five minutes. These small shifts didn't just change my habits, they changed how I experienced life And what do these habits lead to? Clarity.

Clarity is like that first deep breath after a storm when the air feels fresh and alive. It's the moment the fog lifts, and you can finally see the path ahead. For me, clarity isn't about having all the answers, it's about that deep, undeniable knowing in my gut that I'm exactly where I'm meant to be. It's like driving through an overcast day and suddenly rounding a corner to find sunlight spilling across the road. Or when the rain washes away the dust and noise, leaving behind a sparkling, clear surface. Clarity doesn't always come with a loud announcement; sometimes, it's a quiet whisper, a subtle shift. But when it arrives, you feel it.

Clarity doesn't always come from quiet reflection, it can also come from reaching out. Sometimes, a conversation with a coach, mentor, or trusted friend can be the flashlight that illuminates the corners of your thoughts. These conversations have been game-changing for me, offering new perspectives and helping me realign with my path. If you're feeling stuck, don't hesitate to seek support. A coach or mentor can help you ask the right questions, clear the mental clutter, and rediscover your inner knowing. Clarity isn't something you have to find alone, it's something you create, often in connection with others.

Habits and clarity go hand in hand. When you build meaningful habits, you create the space to listen to your inner voice. You quiet the monkey mind, making room for clarity to emerge. It's not about chasing clarity but allowing it to flow into your life naturally, like sunlight breaking through the clouds. By stacking habits that nurture your mind, body, and spirit, you create a foundation for intentional living. As my mentor Lisa always says, "Chop Wood, Carry Water". These small, consistent actions invite clarity into your life, helping you navigate with confidence and ease. In those moments, the path becomes illuminated, and you realize that everything you need has been within you all along.

Mentors, Guides, and Experts

Lisa Carpenter

Lisa Carpenter is a coach who brings deep clarity and perspective to both life and business. When I worked with Lisa, she helped me see through the chaos and find a path that aligned with my true values and goals. Her ability to cut through emotional fog and offer practical, yet heart-centered guidance gave me the tools to step into my purpose with confidence. Lisa's approach is intuitive, empowering, and deeply transformative, working with her has been a pivotal turning point in my personal and professional life.

lisacarpenter.ca

James Wedmore

James Wedmore, host of the Mind Your Business podcast, brings a refreshing and transformative approach to entrepreneurship. His focus on the intersection of business strategy and personal growth has been instrumental in shifting how I approach both my work and my mindset. Through his teachings, I learned that success isn't just about the hustle, it's about aligning your inner world with the external actions you take. James' guidance helped me build a business that not only thrives but feels in tune with who I am at my core.

jameswedmoretraining.com

Jim Fortin

Jim Fortin, with his transformational coaching program (TCP), has a way of helping you see beyond the surface of your life and business. Working with Jim allowed me to understand that real transformation starts from within, shifting the beliefs and subconscious patterns that hold us back. Through his teachings, I learned how to break through my limitations and step into a higher version of myself, not just in business but in every aspect of life. His methods are a true blend of mindset, spirituality, and action.

jimfortin.com

NOTES

MOON

WHISPERED WORDS

Stepping outside, she feels it instantly, a magnetic tug, subtle but irresistible, pulling her gaze upward. Her chin tilts as if guided by unseen hands, and there it is: the moon, radiant and luminous, casting her world in shimmering silver. She doesn't just see its light; she feels it, a quiet pulse echoing in time with her own. It's an ancient thrill, a spark that hums through her being, illuminating her from within.

A soft smile curls across her lips. When the moon greets you before dawn, she thinks, it's no coincidence, it's a sign. A promise that today holds something magickal.

Her bond with the moon is not new. It's as if the rhythm of its cycles is etched into her soul, a melody that plays endlessly in her heart. With each New Moon, she feels a gentle invitation, a whispered nudge to pause, to breathe, to retreat inward. The darkness of the moon mirrors her own moments of stillness, the unknown spaces within her where dreams stir and intentions take root. It's a time to wipe the slate clean, to plant seeds in the fertile soil of possibility.

She breathes deeply, feeling the quiet power of beginnings, sensing that she, too, is on the cusp of something new.

Then, as the moon grows, so does she. When it becomes full, brilliant and unyielding, its light touches every corner of her being. She feels her emotions rise with the tides, raw and unfiltered, demanding her attention. The energy is electric, alive, illuminating the hidden places she so often avoids. The Full Moon is a time of truth, a mirror held high. Beneath its glow, she surrenders, releasing what no longer serves her. She lets go, not with sadness, but with gratitude, clearing space for what's yet to come.

In the moon's radiance, she feels a profound truth: she is wild and resilient, as untamed as the tides, as eternal as the cycle that binds them.

What is it about the moon that transforms everything? That makes her heart swell with a sense of boundlessness, of mystery? Perhaps it's the knowing, the quiet, steady knowing, that this celestial light will always return. It will always rise, always pull, always shine, no matter the shadows that try to obscure it.

The moon, in all its phases, reflects her own. Whether waxing or waning, in darkness or in light, it reminds her that she, too, holds endless cycles within herself. Each one sacred. Each one powerful. Each one hers.

The Magick and Mystery of the Moon

The moon has always been one of my first loves in the realm of the mystical. There's something about its quiet power, hanging high in the sky, that feels alive and deeply connected to everything we are. Have you ever taken a moment to really look at it, just before darkness falls, as its soft light begins to blanket the earth? Or in those quiet, early morning hours, when the world hasn't quite woken up, and the moon smiles down at you like an old friend? It's in those moments that I feel its magick most deeply. Sometimes, it's as simple as glancing up and just knowing, today is going to be a good day.

I once read something that stuck with me, perfectly capturing why the moon resonates so deeply:

"When you remember that the moon controls the changing tides of the ocean, you also have to remind yourself that we as human beings are made up of over 60% water and we, too, are susceptible to its changing phases. So when you let the lunar cycles act as a framework for your daily life, you may start to tap into its powerful energy and begin to manifest more than ever before by simply aligning with the right times to plan, act, and observe."

And that's just it, the moon's pull isn't just a force of nature; it's a force within us, too. It's hard to explain exactly why it captivates me, but I feel its energy in my bones. It's a knowing, one I want to share with you in the hopes that you might feel it too. The moon has a way of showing up when we need it most, as if to remind us that we are never truly alone in our transformation.

Lunar Wisdom and the Cycles of Life

Throughout time, the moon has enchanted humanity, its phases acting as a cosmic rhythm for both our external lives and inner worlds. Each of the thirteen lunar cycles in a year carries its own unique energy, mirroring themes of renewal, growth, release, and reflection. These cycles offer a framework to explore our emotional and spiritual landscapes, helping us align with the natural flow of life.

The 13 Moon Calendar, a system of timekeeping rooted in ancient traditions, breaks the year into thirteen months of 28 days, syncing closely with the moon's phases. This lunar rhythm invites a more intuitive relationship with time, one that honors our need for rest, creativity, and healing. Native American and Celtic traditions revered this connection, celebrating the synchronicity between lunar cycles and women's menstrual rhythms as a sacred bond with nature. In these cultures, the moon wasn't just a light in the sky; it was a living presence, a grandmother, a storyteller, a keeper of the sacred.

The Moon and the Feminine Archetypes

The moon has long been a symbol of the sacred feminine. Across cultures and lineages, its phases have mirrored the energetic rhythms of womanhood: birth, growth, decline, and rebirth. These rhythms are reflected in the Triple Goddess archetype: Maiden, Mother, and Crone.

The Maiden aligns with the waxing moon. She is youth, potential, curiosity, and becoming. This is the spark of life, the daring dreamer, the one just beginning.

The Mother reflects the full moon. She is fertile, creative, and whole. She carries wisdom and nurtures both life and vision. Her light is steady, expansive, and magnetic.

The Crone arrives with the waning moon and dark moon. She is the keeper of mysteries, the wise one, the teacher of release and transformation. Her energy teaches us that letting go is not an ending, but a sacred beginning.

These archetypes are not just stages of life, but phases we move through in cycles; monthly, emotionally, and energetically. No matter your gender, these feminine archetypes live within you. They show up in your creativity, your boundaries, your intuition, your healing. The moon becomes a mirror, reflecting which version of yourself is asking to lead, to rest, to rise.

To live in tune with the moon is to honor the sacred feminine, not as something weak or passive, but as something powerful, cyclical, and alive. It reminds us that we are not meant to be linear, productive machines. We are meant to ebb, to flow, to feel, to know.

The Eight Phases of the Moon

The moon's cycle is a story told in eight chapters, each one offering its own energy and wisdom:

- **New Moon:** In the dark stillness, new seeds are planted. This is a time for setting intentions, dreaming, and envisioning what's to come. It asks us to trust in beginnings, even when we can't yet see the outcome.
- **Waxing Crescent:** As the first sliver of light appears, it's time to gather resources and begin laying the foundation for your goals. This is the spark phase, where hope meets action.

- **First Quarter:** The moon is half-lit, encouraging action and persistence. Challenges may arise, but they're the stepping stones to growth. This is where you choose your path and commit.
- **Waxing Gibbous:** With the moon nearly full, refine your intentions and prepare for their fruition. This is a time for adjustment, detail work, and patience as things come into alignment.
- **Full Moon:** A time of culmination, celebration, and illumination. Reflect on what has manifested and let the moon's energy amplify your gratitude and release. Emotions may rise, but they bring clarity.
- **Waning Gibbous:** As the light begins to fade, turn inward with gratitude. Let go of anything that no longer serves you. Integrate the lessons.
- **Last Quarter:** The shadow grows, inviting forgiveness and cleansing. This is a powerful time for breaking patterns and resetting the soul.
- **Waning Crescent:** Rest, reflect, and gather your energy for the next cycle. This is a sacred pause before the new moon begins again. Honor your need for quiet.

Each phase offers an invitation to flow with the cosmic rhythm, enriching both your spiritual practice and daily life. When you live in sync with the moon, life stops feeling like a straight line and begins to feel like a spiral, ever deepening, ever revealing.

Rituals to Connect with the Moon

One of my favorite ways to honor the moon is through ritual. Ritual doesn't have to be complicated or formal; it just has to be yours. I've participated in moon circles with others, and I've also created quiet, solitary moments under the moonlight that felt just as sacred.

New Moon Rituals: These are about beginnings and intention-setting. Light a candle, write down your dreams, and plant seeds—literally or metaphorically. Let the darkness of the new moon hold your desires as they begin to take root. Align your intentions with the zodiac energy of the moon; for example, a New Moon in Aries is perfect for bold action, while a New Moon in Cancer encourages emotional healing and nurturing.

Full Moon Rituals: These rituals are about release and reflection. Place your crystals under the moonlight to cleanse them, write down what you're ready to let go of, and burn it as a symbolic act of release. A Full Moon in Scorpio might guide you to dive deep into transformation, while a Full

Moon in Taurus invites grounding and gratitude. Don't be afraid to cry, dance, laugh, howl; whatever your body asks for, let it move through you. Your ritual is your return to self. A chance to realign, remember, and reclaim.

The Moon's Influence on Us

The moon's power isn't just spiritual, it's physical too. Ancient philosophers like Pliny the Elder spoke of the moon's ability to "penetrate all things," influencing tides, plants, animals, and even humans. And while modern science may not explain all the magick, it does back some of it. Studies show that the full moon can disrupt our sleep patterns, we take longer to fall asleep, experience less deep sleep, and often wake up feeling less rested.

And its power doesn't stop there. The moon played a role in freeing the massive Ever Given cargo ship stranded in the Suez Canal, when the supermoon's strong tidal pull helped shift the ship and clear one of the world's busiest waterways. If the moon can move oceans and global trade, imagine what it can do within us.

The moon is more than just a celestial body; she is a whisper from the universe, a quiet companion in our most honest moments. A mirror to our own becoming, waxing and waning with our joy, our grief, our growth. Her cycles remind us that we are allowed to begin again and again, that stillness has a purpose, that release is holy, and that light always returns. Her magick isn't loud or performative; it's steady, ancient, and deeply personal. All you have to do is look up and remember who you are.

Mentors, Guides, and Experts

Ichel Francis

Ichel Francis, also known as The Moon Goddess, creates a sacred space for deep connection and self-reflection through her Moon Circles. Being part of her Moon Circle allowed me to connect more deeply with lunar energy, using the cycles of the moon as a guide for personal transformation. Ichel's wisdom and her nurturing, intuitive presence helped me align with the natural ebb and flow of life, bringing a sense of rhythm and grounding into both my spiritual practice and daily life.

ichelfrancis.com

Yasmin Boland

Yasmin Boland, the author of Moonology, has been a guiding light in my journey of working with lunar energy. Her books opened up a deeper understanding of the moon's cycles and how they influence every aspect of life. Yasmin's wisdom and practical approach to aligning with the moon's phases helped me cultivate a rhythm in my spiritual practice that feels both grounded and magickal. Her work is an inspiring reminder that the moon holds the key to transformation when we're ready to listen.

yasminboland.com

Spirit Daughter

Jill Wintersteen with the Spirit Daughter brings the power of astrology, moon phases, and intention-setting into daily practice. Through her work, I've learned how to harness the energy of each lunar cycle and astrological movement to create more balance and alignment in my life. Spirit Daughter's guidance, through her beautifully crafted workbooks and insights, has become a part of my ritual, helping me reflect, set intentions, and connect more deeply with the energy of the cosmos. Her approach makes the wisdom of the stars feel both accessible and transformative.

spiritdaughter.com

NOTES

HUMAN DESIGN

Whispered Words

Being open, truly transparent, it isn't easy for her. It feels raw, vulnerable, like stepping into the light after years of hiding in the shadows. But she knows, deep down, that if even one person is touched by her words, if just one finds their own path through hers, then that is the purpose. That is why she steps out, why she allows herself to be seen. No more hiding.

She looks deep within herself and asks the hard questions, the ones that linger like unopened doors in her soul. She faces the truths she's avoided, knowing the answers might change everything. She searches, she seeks, and just when she thinks she's uncovered what she's been looking for, she dives deeper still. This journey was never meant to be easy, and it was never meant to be quick. Growth rarely is.

But little by little, the light begins to break through. At first, it's just a flicker, a glimpse of sunlight breaking through the latticework of leaves or the moon casting its tentative glow from behind a veil of clouds. It's subtle but powerful, a reminder that something waits on the other side of the discomfort.

And then, one day, she feels it: a deep, unshakable knowing.

This is me.
Can you see me?
I am here, showing my true, authentic self.
Not for approval.
Not for acceptance.

But for the peace that blooms within her when she is grounded and rooted in her own truth.

The journey she is on is not a quick fix, but she's found a map leading her back to the self she's always been but never fully embraced. It calls her to peel back the layers of conditioning, to release what isn't hers, and to step boldly into the life that is uniquely hers to live.

It's a path of love, love for the world, for those around her, but most importantly, for herself. The kind of love that doesn't demand perfection but honors the beauty of simply being.

When she begins to live in alignment, it feels like breathing for the first time after holding her breath for far too long. No longer does she search outside herself for validation, answers, or worth. Instead, she finds them within, rooted in the truth of who she is. And in that grounding, she discovers the ultimate love: the love that begins within her and radiates outward, touching everything she encounters.

This is her journey.
This is her truth.
This is her.

Human Design: A Cosmic Treasure Map

Where do I even begin with Human Design? It feels like I've been on this journey forever, peeling back layer after layer, only to discover there's always more to learn. And that's part of the magick, it's vast, intricate, and endlessly fascinating. For me, this system has been like stumbling upon a treasure map. But instead of leading to gold, it leads to something far more valuable: a deeper understanding of myself.

Not just the self the world sees, but the real self. The one underneath the conditioning, the programming, the shoulds. Human Design cracked me open. It was like looking in a mirror that finally reflected who I actually was, not who I'd been trying to be.

I'm a 6/2 Emotional Manifesting Generator. If you're new to Human Design, that probably sounds like a foreign language. Don't worry, I'll explain. But first, let's talk about what Human Design actually is.

Imagine combining astrology, the I Ching, Kabbalah, the chakra system, and quantum physics into one framework. That's Human Design. It's a system that reveals how uniquely we're all wired, offering insight into our strengths, challenges, and how we're meant to operate in the world. It's like being handed the user manual you didn't know you needed for your life.

The Five Types

At the heart of Human Design are five energy types, each with its own way of interacting with the world. Think of them as different roles in a play or pieces of a puzzle, each one essential to the bigger picture:

- **Manifestors:** The fire-starters, here to initiate and inspire. Manifestors don't need permission to act; they're the locomotives that create new paths, sparking movements that others follow. They're not meant to finish everything they start, but their ability to get things moving is unmatched.
- **Generators:** The builders, making up around 70% of the population. They're the powerhouses with sustainable energy, especially when they're doing work they love. Generators thrive on satisfaction, and when they follow what lights them up, their energy becomes magnetic, pulling opportunities and people toward them.
- **Manifesting Generators:** The multitasking dynamos. They're a hybrid of Manifestors and Generators, with the ability to juggle multiple passions and pivot quickly when something no longer serves them.

They move fast and efficiently, blending initiating energy with the sustained power of Generators.

- **Projectors:** The seers, here to guide and direct. Projectors have a natural ability to understand others deeply, making them incredible advisors, leaders, and energy managers. But their magick only shines when they're recognized and invited into the right roles.
- **Reflectors:** The rarest type, Reflectors are the mirrors of their environment. Their energy is fluid, reflecting the health and harmony of the world around them. They thrive when they honor their unique process of waiting a full lunar cycle to make decisions, allowing them to deeply align with their truth.

Each type has its own strategy for moving through life with more ease. Manifestors inform. Generators and Manifesting Generators respond. Projectors wait for the invitation. Reflectors wait for clarity over time. Knowing your type and strategy is like discovering the secret sauce for how you interact with the world and how the world interacts with you.

Authority: Your Inner Compass

Beyond your type, Human Design introduces the concept of Authority, your personal decision-making tool. This is the part of you that knows what's right, even when your mind tries to overthink it.

For some, this might be Emotional Authority, where clarity comes after riding the waves of feelings over time. Others might have Sacral Authority, guided by gut instincts and an immediate "yes" or "no" response. There's also Splenic Authority, rooted in intuition and that quiet inner voice of knowing, and Lunar Authority for Reflectors, which aligns with the cycles of the moon.

Learning to trust your Authority can be life-changing. For me, it meant no longer forcing clarity in the moment. I started giving myself space. I waited. I let the emotional waves roll through me. And slowly, I learned the difference between a reactive choice and a true, grounded yes. It was uncomfortable at first. I'm not naturally patient. But it became sacred. It became mine.

A Cosmic Train: The Types in Action

I love using the analogy of a train to illustrate how Human Design types work together:

Manifestors are the locomotives, setting the train in motion and carving out new tracks. Generators are the engine cars, providing steady, sustainable energy to keep the train moving. Manifesting Generators combine roles, multitasking as both initiators and workers, switching tracks and hauling cargo effortlessly. Projectors are the conductors, guiding and directing the train with wisdom and insight, ensuring everything runs smoothly. Reflectors are the passengers who mirror the train's environment, reflecting whether the journey is harmonious or needs adjustment.

It's not about hierarchy, it's harmony. When each part honors its role, the whole system flows.

Diving Deeper

Of course, this is just the surface of Human Design. Beyond your type and Authority are layers upon layers of insights, including profiles, gates, channels, and centers, all of which add depth to your chart. Your profile, for instance, reveals how you're designed to learn and interact with the world. For me, being a 6/2 means I'm a natural role model, but it didn't start that way. The 6-line life is a three-part journey, and mine came with its fair share of crashing, burning, and rising again.

The "2" in my profile is the hermit. The one who needs solitude, who creates best when she's not trying so hard to be seen. That duality, being a role model and also needing to retreat, wasn't something I always understood. But Human Design helped me make peace with both.

Then there are the gates and channels, which act like pathways of energy, showing where you're naturally gifted and where you might face challenges. Some gates felt like home the first time I read about them. Others felt like hard truths I wasn't ready to face. But every one of them has taught me something about my purpose, my patterns, and my power.

Living Your Design

Human Design isn't about fixing yourself or fitting into a mold. It's about remembering who you are beneath the noise. It's about turning down the volume on what the world says you should be, and turning up the dial on your own frequency. It's not a quick fix. It's a deep return.

Whether you're a Manifestor carving new paths, a Generator following your passions, a Manifesting Generator juggling multiple roles, a Projector guiding others, or a Reflector mirroring the world around you, your design is your unique blueprint.

So, are you ready to explore yours? Start small. Let it be an unfolding. Let it be an invitation. You don't have to decode the whole chart at once. Just begin. Your body remembers. Your energy knows. Your truth is waiting to be lived.

Ready to get started? If you're curious about your own Human Design chart, you can generate it for free online using your birth date, time, and location. But if you want a deeper, more guided experience, I highly recommend connecting with the mentors, guides, and experts I've learned from. You'll find them on the next page: the mentors, guides and experts who hold this work with integrity, depth, and clarity.

This is where your journey begins. Not with answers, but with awareness. Not with certainty, but with curiosity. Let your design reveal itself to you, one layer at a time.

Want to dive deeper into your chart?
There's a whole world of discovery waiting for you.

Mentors, Guides, and Experts

Jenna Zoe

Jenna Zoe, creator of My Human Design, was my first introduction to the world of Human Design. Through her podcast, app, and resources, Jenna makes this system accessible, offering practical insights into how to live in alignment with your unique design. Her teachings helped me understand myself on a deeper level and how to make decisions that feel authentic and right for me. Jenna's work is both grounding and enlightening, allowing me to embrace my true self and navigate life with more ease and purpose.

myhumandesign.com

Emma Dunwoody

Emma Dunwoody, an expert in Human Design, offers a transformative way to understand yourself and how you move through the world. Her work with Human Design opened up a new level of self-awareness for me, blending the spiritual and practical to create deep personal alignment. Emma's guidance helped me discover how to work with my natural energy and decision-making strategies, allowing me to live with more ease and authenticity. Her teachings have been key in helping me understand how to embody my true essence fully.

emmadunwoody.com

Karen Curry Parker

Karen Curry Parker, the creator of Quantum Human Design, introduced me to a deeper layer of Human Design that goes beyond traditional interpretations. Her work integrates a quantum perspective, helping to expand the possibilities of who we can become when we align with our true energetic blueprint. Through her teachings, I learned how to tap into higher potentials within my design, using this knowledge to unlock personal transformation. Karen's insights helped me see Human Design as a living, evolving tool for both spiritual growth and practical application.

quantumhumandesign.com

NOTES

TAROT & ORACLE

WHISPERED WORDS

Excitement mingled with a tinge of apprehension hums through her veins as she wakes. Will today be the day it all falls apart, or the day it fits together? A dark and morbid thought, perhaps, but truthful nonetheless.

Throwing her legs over the side of the bed, she stretches, letting the cool air pull her fully into wakefulness. She stumbles toward the bathroom, wiping sleep from her eyes. Not today, she thinks. Today will not be the day it all falls apart. Today is the day it all comes together.

Still moving through the haze of morning, she walks silently into the kitchen, leaving the harsh overhead light off. In the soft shadows, she pours the coffee beans into the grinder. The sound is sharp and familiar, grounding her, pulling her further into the rhythm of the day. They say this is the best way to start the morning, she thinks with a small smile, and maybe they're right.

Cup in hand, she sinks into the worn leather chair by the window, its cushions molded perfectly to her form from years of use. Pulling back the curtains, she lets the golden light of dawn spill into the room. The sun, just beginning its climb over the bluff, casts a shimmering path across the lake, making the water look like liquid gold. She lifts her steaming cup to her lips, savoring the quiet, the stillness, the peace.

Her fingers drift to the oracle deck resting on the small table beside her. She picks it up reverently, feeling the familiar weight of it in her hands. Closing her eyes, she takes a deep breath and sets her intention.

"What does my soul need to know today?" she whispers softly into the stillness.
She shuffles the cards slowly, letting their energy mingle with hers. One card leaps from the deck, landing face down on her lap. She smiles, a knowing smile, as she turns it over. The image feels like a whisper from the universe, a gentle nudge in the direction of her truth.

In this moment, the pieces feel like they're coming together. The sunlight, the coffee, the cards, they weave a quiet spell around her, grounding her in the here and now. The question no longer lingers: whether today will break her or build her. Instead, she knows. Today is exactly as it is.

Exploring Tarot and Oracle Magick

What exactly are tarot and oracle cards you ask? Well, they are a tool that help you gain clarity around a situation or circumstance. Tarot cards offer a rich, symbolic journey into self-awareness, blending centuries-old wisdom with personal intuition. Originating as playing cards in 15th-century Europe, they evolved by the 18th century into a mystical tool for divination. The deck is divided into the Major Arcana, which represents significant life themes and spiritual lessons, and the Minor Arcana, focusing on everyday experiences through four suits: Wands (creativity and action), Cups (emotions and relationships), Swords (challenges and intellect), and Pentacles (material aspects and career).

When you use tarot, it's like holding a mirror up to your inner world. You start by forming a question or focus area in your mind, then shuffle the deck while concentrating on this intention. After that, you draw cards in a specific spread, like the three-card spread to explore past, present, and future influences, or the Celtic Cross for a deeper dive. The cards drawn, whether from the Major or Minor Arcana, are rich with symbols and imagery that tap into your subconscious, offering insights that reflect your current life situation or emotional state.

Each card tells part of a story, providing guidance, revealing hidden truths, or offering new perspectives. For instance, pulling The Fool might suggest the beginning of a new journey, while The Tower could indicate sudden change or upheaval. The Minor Arcana, divided into the suits of Wands, Cups, Swords, and Pentacles, helps you explore more specific areas of your life, like creativity, emotions, challenges, or material concerns.

But tarot isn't about predicting the future with certainty; it's more like having a conversation with your higher self. The cards provide a reflective practice that helps you navigate life's complexities, offering clarity and insight into your decisions and personal growth. Whether you're seeking guidance on a particular issue or just wanting to connect more deeply with your inner wisdom, tarot serves as a powerful tool to explore the unseen and understand the energies shaping your journey.

Starting your journey with tarot is like opening a door to an ancient, mystical world. It begins with feeling a connection to a deck that speaks to you, let the imagery, the energy, draw you in. As you lay out the cards, listen not just with your mind, but with your spirit. Tarot is an art that blends knowledge with intuition; it's a dance between you and the cards, where each symbol whispers secrets from the universe. Embrace the mystery, practice with an open heart, and let the wisdom of the cards unfold naturally. As you deepen your relationship with the tarot, you'll find that it's not about memorizing meanings but about letting the cards guide you through the unseen currents of life. Trust your inner voice, and over time, your readings will become a true reflection of the mystical connection between you and the divine.

While Tarot cards open the door to a structured, ancient system of wisdom, a language steeped in symbolism and archetypes that guide us through life's mysteries. Oracle cards, on the other hand, feel like a breath of fresh air, less structured, more fluid, and deeply personal. Where tarot provides a map, oracle cards feel like a conversation, an open-ended dialogue with the universe that shifts and flows with your energy in the moment.

Tarot to Oracle: A New Way to Listen

Transitioning from tarot to oracle cards is like moving from a classical symphony to an improvised melody, both beautiful, both powerful, but each offering a unique experience. While tarot asks you to dive deep into its archetypal language, oracle cards invite you to listen to the voice of your intuition with fewer boundaries. They're not meant to replace tarot but to complement it, offering messages that are just as profound but often simpler to interpret. Let's explore how oracle cards create this sacred space for connection and how they can enhance your spiritual practice in their own unique way.

To begin your journey with oracle cards, approach them as if you're opening a doorway to a sacred conversation with the universe. Choose a deck that resonates deeply with your soul, let the artwork, energy, and theme draw you in. When you're ready, create a quiet, sacred space. Hold the deck in your hands, infuse it with your intention, and ask for guidance. Gently shuffle the cards, allowing your intuition to guide you to the ones that hold the message you need to hear. Trust in the wisdom that flows through, knowing that each card reveals the energies at play in your life. Oracle cards are your spiritual companions, offering insight, clarity, and a deeper connection to the unseen realms.

Tarot and oracle cards each offer their own unique magick, yet both are tools for connection, reflection, and guidance. Tarot provides a structured framework, steeped in ancient wisdom, while oracle cards offer fluidity and intuitive freedom. Together, they create a beautiful balance, one grounded in tradition, the other in personal expression. Whether you choose one or both, the true power lies in how you use them to deepen your connection with yourself and the universe. They are mirrors for the soul, offering clarity, insight, and a touch of divine wisdom to guide you on your journey. Trust in the process, and let the cards reveal the path that's always been waiting for you.

Mentors, Guides & Experts

Minnow Pond

Chris, the creator of Minnow Pond Tarot, brings a blend of intuition and practicality to his tarot and oracle card readings. His guidance has been a go-to for me when seeking clarity on various aspects of life, from love and career to personal growth. Through his YouTube channel, Chris offers insightful, grounded interpretations that resonate deeply, helping to illuminate the hidden energies at play. His readings always leave me feeling more empowered and aligned, making tarot accessible and transformational for everyday life.

minnowpond.com

Angi Sullins

Angi Sullins, the creator of the W.I.T.C.H. Oracle deck, has crafted a tool that weaves together mysticism, empowerment, and deep self-reflection. Her deck has become a favorite of mine, offering not just guidance but a powerful reminder of the magick that lies within. Angi's vision with W.I.T.C.H. taps into the wild, intuitive nature in all of us, making each card a call to connect more deeply with ourselves and the unseen forces around us. Her work inspires clarity, empowerment, and soulful transformation.

angisullins.com

Hay House

Hay House is a well-known publisher and resource for those seeking spiritual tools, including tarot and oracle decks. Their collection features works from renowned spiritual teachers, offering a wide range of decks that support personal growth, intuition, and clarity. Whether you're just starting with oracle or tarot, or you're deepening your existing practice, Hay House offers something for everyone. I've found some of my favorite decks through them, and their selection continues to inspire and empower my spiritual journey.

hayhouse.com

NOTES

SEASONS & FESTIVALS

Whispered Words

The seasons come alive in her hands like threads of a spinning wheel, weaving a story only the earth remembers. She feels the pull of time's dance, each moment tied to the next, a cycle she knows by heart but still marvels at with each turn.

Spring whispers to her first, its voice soft and sweet as wildflowers unfurl. She kneels in the garden, soil pressed between her fingers, planting tiny seeds with quiet hope. The mornings are still cool, but the sun's kiss lingers longer each day. Beltane arrives in a wild rush of color and flame. She lights candles on her windowsill, her heart beating in rhythm with the crackle of unseen bonfires, as though she can hear the ancient songs in the wind.

Summer strides in, bold and radiant, drenching the world in golden light. She stretches her arms to the sun, feeling its heat sink deep into her skin. The days are long, lazy and electric all at once. She picks berries in the early morning, their sweetness staining her lips, and at sunset, she dances barefoot in the grass to honor the Solstice,her joy spilling out into the twilight like spilled wine.

Autumn tiptoes in with a rustle of leaves, her colors rich and her breath crisp. She wraps herself in a shawl and wanders the forest, gathering acorns and moss-covered twigs, treasures from the earth. At Samhain, she sits by the fire with a mug of spiced cider, writing letters to the ones she's lost. She burns them in the hearth, watching the smoke curl upward as if carrying her words to the stars.

Winter doesn't arrive,it settles, like a snowfall too soft to notice at first. She lights a fire and watches frost etch lace patterns on the windows. At Yule, she hangs garlands of pine and holly, their scent filling the air with promise. She stands beneath the stars on the longest night, hands wrapped around a candle, waiting for the moment she feels the light shift, the quiet knowing that dawn is on its way.

Each season invites her to do something more than live,it asks her to play, to create, to honor the cycles that have carried humanity through countless turns of the wheel. And as she moves through each phase, she feels the quiet magick of it all: the way the earth never truly stops, the way the soul is always in motion, spinning toward its next great story.

Seasons and Festivals: The Wheel of the Year

The Wheel of the Year isn't just a calendar; it's a living, breathing rhythm that invites us to feel more deeply connected to the world and ourselves. It's the pulse beneath the soil, the whisper in the wind, the invitation to slow down and notice. While many of these festivals have been absorbed into modern life, Yule into Christmas, Ostara into Easter, their roots are older, wilder, more sacred. They speak to something ancient within us, something that remembers.

When you follow the Wheel, you're not just celebrating dates. You're aligning with energy, archetypes, and the natural ebb and flow of life. You're remembering how to live in season, not just with the world, but with your own becoming.

Let these festivals become more than markers of time. Let them be portals. Practices. Touchstones. Here's how they unfold...

Yule (Winter Solstice) – The Rebirth of Light
Yule marks the longest night of the year, and with it, the quiet miracle of the sun's return. It's a time of stillness, reflection, and deep inner knowing. Light candles to welcome the light back in, not just in the sky, but in your spirit. Journal by firelight, sip spiced cider, set intentions like seeds beneath snow. Work with Clear Quartz to amplify clarity and vision.

Imbolc – The Spark of Hope
The earth is stirring beneath the frost. Imbolc is a whisper of what's to come, a flicker, a thaw, the promise of possibility. Honor Brigid with firelight, poetry, and small acts of creation. Cleanse your space. Breathe life into dormant dreams. Citrine and Carnelian can help reignite your inner flame.

Ostara (Spring Equinox) – Balance and Renewal
Light and dark are in perfect balance. This is the turning point where green things awaken, and we begin again. Ostara invites you to plant, not just herbs or flowers, but intentions, habits, and hope. Get your hands in the dirt. Decorate eggs. Meditate with Green Aventurine or Rose Quartz and welcome in the softness of new beginnings.

Beltane – The Fire of Passion
Beltane is wild, sensual, alive. A celebration of fertility, creativity, and full-bodied joy. Let your body lead, dance, make love, light a fire.

Adorn your space (and yourself) with flowers. Garnet and Carnelian amplify vitality and desire. This is a festival of aliveness, lean in.

Litha (Summer Solstice) – The Sun at Its Peak
The longest day, the highest sun. Litha is celebration in its purest form. The energy is high and golden, ripe for manifestation and radiance. Swim in lakes. Make flower crowns. Bask unapologetically in your own light. Work with Sunstone or Tiger's Eye for confidence and joy.

Lammas/Lughnasadh – The First Harvest
Here, we begin to gather. Lammas is about gratitude and groundedness. Bake bread, harvest herbs, give thanks. What have you grown this year, tangibly or within? Celebrate it. Let Citrine support your abundance mindset, and take time to reflect on what's been earned through effort.

Mabon (Autumn Equinox) – Balance and Gratitude
Again, the light and dark meet in harmony. Mabon is a time of inner harvest. Look around, what are you carrying? What are you ready to lay down? Spend time in stillness, surrounded by the hues of turning leaves. Let Amethyst or Smoky Quartz help you ground into gratitude and prepare for the descent.

Samhain – The Veil Between Worlds
The final harvest. The gate to the unseen. Samhain is sacred. It invites you to connect with your ancestors, to honor your grief, to dance with the mysteries. Create an altar. Speak their names. Burn what no longer serves. Use Black Tourmaline or Labradorite to move through this threshold with reverence and protection.

The Wheel of the Year is more than seasonal shifts; it's a mirror. Each sabbat reflects something stirring inside you: a call to bloom, to burn, to shed, to rest. This isn't just about following a tradition. It's about remembering a rhythm your soul already knows. So light the candles. Stir the soup. Walk barefoot on the earth. Let the seasons shape you.

Living by the Wheel of the Year isn't about perfection; it's about presence. It's about waking up to the natural rhythms that are already pulsing beneath your daily life and choosing to honor them in your own way. Maybe that looks like planting seeds with intention during Ostara, or writing down what you're ready to release at Samhain. Maybe it's simply pausing to notice the way the light changes through your window, or how your energy rises and falls with the turning of the earth.

You don't need to move to a cottage in the woods or change your whole life. You just need to pay attention. Build small rituals that root you. Let your creativity be guided by the seasons. Reflect in winter. Create in spring. Celebrate in summer. Surrender in autumn. Align your work, your rest, your magick with the movement of the Wheel.

This is a practice of deep listening, not just to nature, but to yourself. The more you live in rhythm with the earth, the more you begin to trust the rhythm within you.

And if you're curious where to begin, look for the festival that speaks to you right now. That's your entry point. The earth will meet you there.

Mentors, Guides, and Experts

Celeste Larsen Mage By Moonlight

Celeste Larsen, the creator of Mage By Moonlight, is a powerful guide for those looking to connect with their inner magick and the ancient energies of the earth. I had the incredible opportunity to journey with her to Scotland, an experience that deepened my connection to both the land and my own spiritual path. Celeste's teachings, woven with lunar magick and deep ancestral wisdom, inspire transformation and healing. She is also the author of Heal the Witch Wound, a book that addresses the collective and personal trauma many feel around reclaiming their power and spiritual gifts. Her work is both empowering and deeply connected to the ancient wisdom of witches and healers, making her a transformative presence in the world of modern spirituality.

magebymoonlight.com

Hannah Hawthorn Simply Witched

Hannah Hawthorn, the creator of Simply Witched, is a modern witch who blends the mystical with the everyday. Her approach to witchcraft is grounded, accessible, and full of practical magick, making it easy for anyone to incorporate witchcraft into their daily life. Through her work, Hannah offers guidance on how to harness your own personal power, work with lunar cycles, and embrace the magick that exists all around you. Her fresh, intuitive style brings a modern twist to ancient practices, making witchcraft a tool for both spiritual growth and everyday empowerment.

simplywitched.com

NOTES

ASTROLOGY

WHISPERED WORDS

She woke with a start, her heart racing like a drumbeat echoing through her chest. Energy coursed through her veins, a surge she couldn't quite place. *What day is it? Where am I?* For a moment, everything felt urgent, unfamiliar. Slowly, she sank back into the mattress, the soft warmth of the blankets grounding her. There was no deadline, no agenda waiting to press her into motion. Her breath steadied, her heart slowed, but her mind had already stirred.

Sleep would not return.

"Good morning, God. Good morning, ancestors, spirit guides, angels," she whispered, her voice soft but certain. It was her ritual, her tether to the day ahead. Slipping out of bed quietly, she moved with care, not wanting to disturb him. Not because she didn't want to share this moment, but because the stillness of the morning, when the world was hers alone, felt sacred.

In those precious, solitary minutes, she heard nothing but her own heartbeat and the whispers of Spirit. The greetings that came back to her, silent and felt, filled her soul in a way words could never describe. They were holy, untouchable moments, a communion so raw and true, it was as though she'd reached across the veil and touched eternity.
But not every morning unfolded with such grace. Some began in chaos, the chatter of her mind drowning out the whispers of her soul. Business plans, unanswered emails, the endless spiral of to-dos. The monkey mind clung tightly, tugging her away from that quiet center.

And yet, the magick was never far.

All it took was one quiet moment to call her back, a step into the cool grass, her bare feet reconnecting with the earth. A deep breath. A whispered "thank you" offered to the universe. Gratitude pouring from her like sunlight through leaves.

In those moments, she could feel it, the spark of life, the rhythm of something eternal flowing through her veins. It was then, and only then, that the true magick happened. The kind that rooted her, lifted her, and reminded her that every day, every breath, could be a beginning.

Understanding Astrology's Influence

Have you ever heard someone groan, 'Mercury must be in retrograde' when their phone glitches or travel plans go haywire? Or maybe you've seen memes blaming the stars for the day's chaos? It's easy to laugh it off, but astrology is more than just cosmic scapegoating. It's a tool, an ancient practice, that taps into the rhythms of the universe and, when used with intention, can offer profound insights into our lives. Let's explore how the planets and stars shape the energy around us.

Astrology is the study of how the movements of celestial bodies, planets, stars, and the moon, affect our lives and the world around us. It's more than just horoscopes or birth charts; it's a cosmic language that helps us understand ourselves and our place in the universe. Each planet, sign, and house has its own energy, shaping different aspects of our personality, emotions, and experiences. When we learn to read this language, we begin to see the deeper connections between the cosmos and our everyday lives. Whether it's Mercury Retrograde throwing us curveballs or the moon influencing our emotions, astrology helps us tap into those universal currents and use them to navigate life more intentionally.

Incorporating astrology into your personal practice allows you to understand your strengths, challenges, and natural rhythms. The natal chart, a snapshot of the sky at the exact moment of your birth, offers a blueprint for understanding your soul's journey. By working with transits, planetary cycles, and even the moon's phases, you can align your actions, intentions, and rituals with the greater energies at play.

The Planets: Cosmic Influencers

Each planet represents a different type of energy or influence in astrology. These energies are not just abstract forces but are tied to distinct aspects of our lives. In your natal chart, where the planets were located at the moment of your birth has a profound impact on your personality, behaviors, and life path.

- **The Sun:** The sun represents your core identity, your essence. It's like the engine that drives you and gives you life force. The sun governs how you express yourself, where you find vitality, and what drives you at your deepest level. It's the sign most people are familiar with because it determines your zodiac "sun sign." If you're a Leo, your sun is in Leo, and this energy is dominant in your personality. The sun's placement in your chart shows your true self and how you shine in the world.

- **The Moon:** If the sun is the core, the moon is the heart. The moon governs your emotions, inner world, and instinctual responses. It's tied to your emotional needs, how you nurture yourself, and how you feel safe. While the sun is outward and expressive, the moon is deeply personal and reflects the part of you that needs care and emotional fulfillment. The moon sign in your chart reveals how you react on an emotional level, how you relate to others on a deeper plane, and what makes you feel secure. For example, a moon in Cancer suggests a deeply nurturing, home-loving energy, while a moon in Aquarius might bring a need for emotional detachment and intellectual stimulation.

- **Mercury:** Mercury is the planet of communication, thought processes, and mental agility. It influences how you think, learn, and express yourself. When Mercury is retrograde (as we often hear about), communication tends to go awry, technology fails, travel plans fall apart, and misunderstandings arise. In your natal chart, Mercury's placement affects how you process information and communicate with others. For example, someone with Mercury in Gemini may have quick, adaptable thoughts, while someone with Mercury in Taurus may be more methodical in their thinking.

- **Venus:** Venus represents love, beauty, and harmony. It governs how you approach relationships, what you find attractive, and how you express affection. In your chart, Venus tells the story of how you give and receive love, your values in relationships, and what brings you pleasure. Someone with Venus in Libra might seek balance and fairness in relationships, while Venus in Scorpio craves deep, transformative connections.

- **Mars:** Mars is the planet of action, desire, and drive. It governs how you assert yourself, your sexual energy, and your ambition. Mars's placement in your chart shows how you go after what you want, where your passions lie, and how you handle conflict. Mars in Aries is fiery and direct, whereas Mars in Pisces might pursue goals more subtly, guided by intuition.

- **Jupiter:** Jupiter is the planet of expansion, luck, and higher learning. It represents where you experience growth and abundance in life. Jupiter's placement indicates how you seek wisdom, where you find joy, and how you attract good fortune. A person with Jupiter in Sagittarius might thrive in travel and philosophical pursuits, while Jupiter in Capricorn could bring success through hard work and discipline.

- **Saturn:** Saturn is the taskmaster of the zodiac, governing discipline, responsibility, and life's challenges. It teaches us through limitations and hardships, showing where we need structure and self-control. In your natal chart, Saturn's placement points to areas of life where you may face obstacles but also where you can achieve mastery through perseverance. Saturn in Virgo, for example, could bring lessons around health, work, and attention to detail, while Saturn in Aquarius might challenge you to break free from outdated social norms.
- **Uranus:** Uranus brings change, rebellion, and innovation. It governs sudden shifts, breakthroughs, and where we seek freedom from convention. In your chart, Uranus reveals where you're meant to disrupt the status quo and embrace individuality. Uranus in Scorpio might bring transformative changes in areas related to intimacy and power, while Uranus in Gemini could manifest through innovation in communication and technology.
- **Neptune:** Neptune governs dreams, intuition, and spirituality. It represents where we connect with the unseen, the mystical, and where we might experience confusion or illusions. Neptune in your chart shows where you're drawn to transcendence, creativity, and compassion, but also where you might struggle with seeing things clearly. Neptune in Pisces, for instance, might give a natural spiritual connection, while Neptune in Capricorn could manifest as illusions about authority and career.
- **Pluto:** Pluto is the planet of transformation, power, and rebirth. It represents deep change, where we confront our shadows, and the areas of life where we're meant to evolve. Pluto in your chart shows where you'll experience profound shifts, letting go of old identities or habits to embrace something new. Pluto in Sagittarius might transform beliefs and philosophies, while Pluto in Leo can bring transformative challenges around self-expression and leadership.

The Signs: Personality and Expression

The planets are the "what," but the zodiac signs are the "how." Each planet's influence is colored by the sign it's in. For instance, Venus in Aries acts differently than Venus in Taurus. The signs represent the different archetypal energies and are divided into elements: fire, earth, air, and water.

- **Fire Signs (Aries, Leo, Sagittarius):** These are the passionate, dynamic, and action-oriented signs. They express energy through excitement, creativity, and enthusiasm.

- **Earth Signs (Taurus, Virgo, Capricorn):** Earth signs are grounded, practical, and focused on the physical world. They express energy through stability, responsibility, and material achievements.
- **Air Signs (Gemini, Libra, Aquarius):** Air signs are intellectual, social, and communicative. They express energy through ideas, conversation, and mental pursuits.
- **Water Signs (Cancer, Scorpio, Pisces):** Water signs are emotional, intuitive, and sensitive. They express energy through feelings, creativity, and deep connections.

The Houses: Areas of Life

The planets and signs tell you what and how, but the houses tell you where in your life these energies play out. Your natal chart is divided into 12 houses, each representing a different area of life.

- **1st House:** The self, appearance, and how you project yourself into the world.
- **2nd House:** Values, money, and personal resources.
- **3rd House:** Communication, siblings, and short journeys.
- **4th House:** Home, family, and roots.
- **5th House:** Creativity, children, and self-expression.
- **6th House:** Work, health, and daily routines.
- **7th House:** Partnerships, marriage, and one-on-one relationships.
- **8th House:** Transformation, death, shared resources, and intimacy.
- **9th House:** Higher learning, philosophy, and travel.
- **10th House:** Career, reputation, and public life.
- **11th House:** Friendships, groups, and aspirations.
- **12th House:** The subconscious, hidden things, and spirituality.

Each house adds a new dimension to the planetary placements. For example, if your Mars is in the 10th house, you might find your ambition and drive are most apparent in your career. If your moon is in the 4th house, your emotional fulfillment might be closely tied to your home and family life.

The Dance of the Sun, Moon, and Rising

Beyond the planets, your Sun, Moon, and Rising sign (the sign that was on the horizon when you were born) are often called the "big three" in astrology, as they shape the core of your personality.

- **Sun:** Your identity and ego. The essence of who you are.
- **Moon:** Your emotional core, reflecting your inner world and needs.
- **Rising:** How you present yourself to the world, your outward persona.

Together, these three signs blend to form a more complete picture of who you are and how you interact with the world around you. Astrology, with its intricate interplay of planets, signs, and houses, offers an entire cosmic language for understanding yourself and your place in the universe. By exploring these energies, you can connect to deeper layers of your psyche, tap into your strengths, and navigate life's challenges with greater awareness. Whether you're working with your Sun sign's drive, your Moon's emotional needs, or your Rising sign's public face, astrology invites you to dance with the cosmos and embrace the patterns that shape your journey.

Ultimately, astrology reminds us that we are part of something bigger, a cosmic dance that connects us not only to the stars but also to each other. When you align with the rhythms of the planets, you start to move with the flow of the universe, understanding that everything is interconnected.

Mentors, Guides, and Experts

Dianna Sab - Voice of the Sacred

Dianna Sab, creator of Voice of the Sacred, is a master of blending astrology with spiritual wisdom. I've had the privilege of taking her astrology course, which has been a transformative journey into understanding how the stars and planets influence every aspect of life. Dianna's teachings go beyond just learning astrology, she helps you tap into the sacred, cosmic rhythms that guide us all, offering deep insights into how you can align with your personal astrological blueprint. Her approach is both intuitive and deeply grounded, making the complex world of astrology feel accessible and life-changing.

voiceofthesacred.com

Astro Consciousness

Mildred Murillo, or Milly, the force behind Astro Consciousness, has been my trusted guide for annual astrology readings. As a psychospiritual astrologer, she blends the wisdom of archetypal astrology with psychology and spirituality, creating deeply insightful sessions that go beyond surface-level astrology. Her readings have provided me with invaluable clarity and tools for navigating life, offering both personal empowerment and a profound connection to my soul's purpose. Milly's work is a transformative experience that has become an essential part of my journey.

astroconsciousness.com

NOTES

SHAMANISM

WHISPERED WORDS

Lying still, she breathes deeply, feeling the rise and fall of her chest as she centers herself. She calls to her guides, their presence a soft hum in the edges of her awareness, inviting them to walk with her on this sacred journey. The drum begins its steady rhythm, low and powerful, like the heartbeat of the earth itself. With each beat, her breath slows, her heart aligns, and her spirit begins to move.

She finds herself standing at the edge of a vast, still lake. The water glimmers under a sky caught between day and night. Waiting there is a small wooden boat and its silent boatman, his face hidden in shadow but his energy calm and knowing. One foot steps into the boat, the other still on the shore, a moment of hesitation. She draws in a deep, steadying breath, surrendering to the pull of the journey, and steps fully aboard.

The boat glides across the lake, each pull of the oar slicing through the water with a soothing rhythm. The journey feels timeless, yet fleeting, the far shore drawing closer with every stroke. When the boat finally touches land, she steps out, her feet meeting solid ground. Waiting for her is a woman cloaked in white, her presence as luminous as the moon. There's an air of expectancy about her, as though she's been waiting for this moment for centuries.

Without a word, they walk together into the woods, where time feels suspended and the air hums with unseen magick. The forest wraps around them, its sounds enveloping her, the gentle rustle of leaves, the murmur of the wind as it whispers through the branches, and the distant trill of birds. A moth dances in the air around her, its fluttering movements light and deliberate. She senses it is no ordinary creature but a guide, sent to help her see what she cannot yet understand.

The woman in white stops in a sunlit clearing, the golden light pooling at their feet. She turns, her voice soft yet filled with ancient knowing. "This is for you," she says, her hand gesturing to the stillness around them. "The answers you seek will come when you are ready." The words settle over her like the warmth of a long-forgotten memory. She feels the truth of them sink into her bones. The forest seems to hold its breath for a moment, and then the world stirs again. Her journey has only just begun.

Connecting with Spirit: The Essence of Shamanism

Shamanism is not a belief system, it's a direct experience. One that begins not with dogma or doctrine, but with the quiet decision to listen. To the wind, to your body, to your ancestors, to the drumbeat of the earth beneath your feet. It is one of the oldest spiritual paths on the planet, rooted in the understanding that everything has spirit and that healing happens when we remember how to speak with the world around us.

At its core, shamanism teaches us this: we are not separate. We are woven into the fabric of life, tethered by breath, energy, and memory to every tree, every animal, every whisper from the unseen. Shamans, whether born into lineage or called through experience, are those who walk between worlds. They gather knowledge, tend to wounds, restore what has been lost. They are seers, healers, messengers, and sometimes, reluctant initiates who've learned through fire and return bearing gifts.

A Brief History of Shamanism

Shamanism predates organized religion by tens of thousands of years. Its traces are found in Paleolithic cave paintings, in the ceremonies of Indigenous tribes across the globe, in the sacred songs and smoke of medicine keepers from Mongolia to the Amazon. While cultures and practices differ, the heart of shamanism remains consistent: the belief in an animate world and our ability to interact with it.

This isn't mythology, it's memory. Something inside us remembers how to sit with the land, how to honor the ancestors, how to dance with spirit. Shamanism is a return, not to a fantasy past, but to a way of being that has never stopped whispering to those willing to listen.

Journeying: The Shaman's Path

Journeying is the sacred practice of stepping beyond the veil,of traveling inward and outward at the same time. Through rhythmic drumming, breathwork, chanting, or movement, the practitioner enters an altered state, where the edges of this world grow soft and the unseen comes forward.

In this space, the journeyer might visit the Lower World, home to animal guides and ancient earth wisdom; the Middle World, a mirror of our waking life, pulsing with plant spirits and ancestral messages; or the Upper World, a realm of high-frequency beings, teachers, and divine archetypes. Each world offers insight, healing, and remembering.

A journey can be profound or subtle. It may bring a symbol, a vision, a deep knowing. The goal is never control,it's connection. You do not command Spirit. You commune with it.

The Language of Nature

In shamanism, nature is both temple and teacher. Every rock, river, and raven holds medicine. The elements, earth, air, fire, and water, are not metaphors but allies. To work with nature in a shamanic way is to enter a conversation: What does the wind want you to hear? What is the lesson in the fire? What story does the tree want to tell you?

Power animals may show up unbidden, through dreams, sightings, or spontaneous knowing. These aren't just symbols. They are spiritual companions with teachings to share. Shamans develop relationships with these beings, learning to walk beside them with humility and reciprocity.

Healing Through Soul Work

In the shamanic view, illness, physical, emotional, or spiritual, is often a symptom of disconnection. Loss of soul parts through trauma, energy intrusions, or forgotten grief can create holes in our being. The role of the shaman is not to "fix" the person, but to restore balance and harmony.

This might involve:

- **Soul Retrieval:** Calling back parts of yourself that splintered during a painful moment.
- **Energy Clearing:** Removing stuck or intrusive energies that are not yours to carry.
- **Extraction:** Gently pulling out what is foreign, toxic, or no longer aligned.
- **Ceremony and Ritual:** Offering the container for transformation through fire, earth, sound, or breath.

True shamanic healing is not quick or linear. It's cyclical. It asks you to participate, to witness your own pain and power, and to step forward as an active co-creator in your healing journey.

Shamanism Today

In modern life, we may not live in small tribes or sit around the village fire, but the call is still there. Many contemporary practitioners honor the ancient ways while adapting them to today's realities. Integrity, cultural respect, and consent are essential. Real shamanic work is not about ego or performance. It's about service, spirit, and showing up with reverence.

People are turning to shamanism not for escape, but for reconnection. In a world that often feels fragmented, it offers a pathway back to wholeness. You don't have to call yourself a shaman to practice these teachings. You only have to be willing to slow down, to listen, and to remember.

Living Shamanically

To live shamanically is to live relationally. It means tending to the invisible as much as the visible. It means creating rituals in daily life, lighting a candle with intention, offering water to a plant, and listening for the message in your dreams.

Start with presence. Build a relationship with the land you're on. Learn its seasons, its spirits. Pay attention to synchronicities. Speak to your ancestors. Say thank you often. Let the sacred be ordinary, and let the ordinary become sacred.

Because in the end, shamanism is not about becoming something new, it's about returning to something ancient inside you that has never truly forgotten the way.

Mentors Guides and Experts

Rhonda McCrimmon - Center for Shamanism

Rhonda McCrimmon, founder of the Center for Shamanism, is a profound guide in the world of shamanic practices. Her teachings on shamanic journeying have opened up new realms of healing and spiritual connection for me, allowing access to deep wisdom through the rhythmic power of the drum. Rhonda's approach is grounded in ancient traditions, yet made accessible for modern spiritual seekers. Through her guidance, I've learned to connect with spirit guides and ancestors, using the drum's heartbeat as a bridge between the physical and spiritual worlds.

centreforshamanism.com

José Luis Stevens - How to Pray the Shaman's Way

José Luis Stevens, PhD, is a renowned shamanic practitioner and co-founder of The Power Path School of Shamanism. With over four decades of experience, he has studied with indigenous shamans worldwide, including a ten-year apprenticeship with a Huichol Marakame in Mexico. His teachings blend ancient wisdom with modern applications, offering profound insights into personal transformation and spiritual growth.

thepowerpath.com/shamanic-education/about-the-power-path/jose-luis-stevens-phd

Don Miguel Ruiz - The Wisdom of the Shamans

Don Miguel Ruiz, renowned author of The Four Agreements, has been a guiding light in the world of personal transformation and spiritual growth. His teachings on breaking limiting beliefs and embracing clarity, love, and truth have profoundly shaped my journey. The wisdom he shares is simple yet deeply transformative, offering practical steps to live with integrity and align with your true self. Don Miguel's work reminds us that true freedom begins within, making his insights timeless and essential for anyone on a metaphysical path.

miguelruiz.com

NOTES

MEDITATION &
BREATHWORK

Whispered Words

She feels it the moment she wakes, today will be a challenge. Grounding feels like chasing shadows, her mind a restless tide that refuses to calm. Energy buzzes in her head, sharp and electric, like distant power lines humming a song she doesn't know the words to. Is it the moon? The shifting energy of the day? Of course, it is. The question is not what, but how, how to flow with it, how to let it charge her rather than scatter her.

She grabs her drum and sinks onto the floor, her body settling into the earth. The drum sits firm in her lap, grounding her, waiting for her touch. She begins with a steady beat, simple and rhythmic, a heartbeat beneath her hands.

One, two, three, four.

She breathes in, long and deep, holding the air as if cradling the universe.

One, two, three, four.

She breathes out, a slow release, like letting go of a heavy weight. With each cycle, time begins to bend and stretch. The static in her mind fades, quieting with every beat of the drum. Her breath and the rhythm become one, a steady dance of sound and stillness.

One, two, three, four.

The beat grows stronger, her hands pressing with intention. The drumming becomes louder, faster, carrying her deeper into herself.

The energy around her shifts. She feels it now, not just in her mind, but in her body. A flow rising from the earth below and pouring down from the heavens above. It moves through her like a river, weaving the elements into her veins. Earth grounds her. Air sharpens her breath. Fire ignites her spirit. Water soothes her edges.

One, two, three, four.

The beat is everything. The rhythm becomes her anchor, her guide, her truth. She feels her body align, her spirit settle, her mind clear. Light *flickers behind her closed eyes, dancing across the quiet landscape of her thoughts. A smile curves at the corners of her lips, soft at first, then stronger.*

All is well.
All is connected.
All is all.

The drumming begins to slow, each beat softer, like footsteps retreating down a familiar path. The buzzing is gone. The hum has stilled. Her breath is quiet, her heart steady, her energy whole.

She rises from the floor with ease, feeling the earth beneath her feet and the sky above her head. The day stretches ahead, waiting for her to step into it, centered, grounded, and ready.

The Art of Stillness: Exploring Meditation and Breathwork

Meditation and breathwork are two of the most powerful tools I've discovered for calming the mind, grounding the body, and connecting with a deeper sense of spiritual awareness. But they're so much more than just a way to relax. These practices help align your energy, clear the mental clutter, and open the door to higher consciousness. Together, they create a profound synergy, grounding you while also elevating your spirit.

Meditation is the art of stillness, a practice that allows us to quiet the mind and turn inward. In those moments of stillness, we tap into a deeper state of awareness. Whether it's through guided visualization, sitting in silence, or focusing on an object or mantra, meditation is a doorway to inner peace, clarity, and connection with your higher self. Breathwork, on the other hand, is a more active practice that uses the power of your breath to shift your physical and energetic state. Through intentional breathing patterns, you can release emotional blockages, re-energize the body, and access altered states of consciousness.

Let's dive into how meditation and breathwork can transform not only your spiritual practice but also the way you navigate your daily life.

The Practice of Meditation

Meditation is often seen as the art of doing nothing, but its real power lies in cultivating an inner stillness that allows us to reconnect with ourselves beyond the noise of everyday life. There are countless forms of meditation, each serving a different purpose, but the essence is the same: to create a moment of presence.

- **Mindfulness Meditation:** This practice encourages awareness of the present moment by focusing on the breath, bodily sensations, or an object. When thoughts arise, they are acknowledged without judgment, and attention is gently brought back to the present. It's incredibly effective for reducing stress and cultivating a sense of calm.
- **Guided Visualization:** In this form, you follow spoken guidance, often visualizing peaceful scenes or sacred spaces. This technique can help enhance your intuition, promote healing, or manifest desires.
- **Loving-Kindness Meditation (Metta):** This heart-centered practice involves directing love and compassion toward yourself, loved ones, and even difficult people in your life. It's deeply healing, helping to

shift old emotional patterns and create a more compassionate state of being.

- **Mantra Meditation:** Here, a word, phrase, or sound is repeated either silently or aloud, which helps to focus the mind. Over time, the repetition of the mantra becomes a vehicle for moving deeper into stillness and connection with higher consciousness.

Through consistent meditation, you begin to peel back the layers of mental chatter and align with a sense of peace and clarity that is always available, waiting beneath the surface.

Breathwork: Breathing Life into Your Practice

Breathwork is an ancient practice that taps into the power of the breath to activate the body's natural ability to heal. By working with intentional breathing patterns, you can calm your mind, shift stuck energy, and create profound emotional and spiritual transformations. Because the breath is directly connected to the nervous system, learning to control it gives you the ability to regulate how you feel in any moment. Breathwork doesn't just calm the surface, it moves energy through the body, clearing emotional and energetic blockages that can hold you back. While meditation often works through the mind, breathwork uses the body as its gateway, opening the door to deep, embodied healing.

- **Conscious Breathing (Pranayama):** In yogic traditions, pranayama is the conscious regulation of the breath to control the life force or prana. Techniques like Nadi Shodhana (alternate nostril breathing) balance the left and right hemispheres of the brain, harmonizing mental and emotional states. Kapalabhati (breath of fire) energizes the body and clears mental fog, while Ujjayi (victorious breath) calms the mind and deepens focus.
- **Box Breathing:** This technique involves inhaling for a count of four, holding for four, exhaling for four, and holding again. It's an incredibly effective way to reduce anxiety, center the mind, and bring yourself back to the present moment.
- **Holotropic Breathwork:** This intense form of breathwork, developed by Stanislav Grof, is used to access non-ordinary states of consciousness. Through deep, rapid breathing, participants often experience deep emotional releases, spiritual awakenings, or profound insights. It's a journey into the depths of the subconscious mind.

- **4-7-8 Breathing:** This technique is designed to quickly calm the nervous system. Inhale through your nose for 4 seconds, hold for 7, and exhale slowly through your mouth for 8 seconds. It's especially helpful in moments of anxiety or before sleep, bringing the body back to a place of deep rest.

Integrating Meditation and Breathwork into Daily Life

The beauty of meditation and breathwork is that they can be incorporated seamlessly into your daily routine. Here are some simple ways to weave these practices into everyday life:

- **Morning Ritual:** Start your day with a 10-minute meditation to set the tone. Combine it with breathwork, such as alternate nostril breathing, to clear any mental fog and energize your mind and body.
- **Grounding Practice:** If you're feeling scattered or overwhelmed during the day, pause for a few minutes and practice box breathing or 4-7-8 breathing to bring your nervous system back into balance. This can be especially helpful before meetings or stressful situations.
- **Evening Wind-Down:** Before bed, engage in a loving-kindness meditation or guided visualization to calm the mind and release the day's tensions. Pair this with deep, slow breathing to help your body enter a state of deep rest.
- **Healing Sessions:** If you're working through deeper emotional or spiritual healing, consider incorporating more intensive breathwork practices like holotropic breathwork or pranayama sessions. These can bring about profound releases, helping you move stagnant energy and process unresolved emotions.

Why Meditation and Breathwork are Essential in Spiritual Practice

The power of both meditation and breathwork lies in their ability to reconnect you with the present moment and the deeper currents of your being. When practiced consistently, they serve as gateways to higher consciousness, emotional healing, and even physical well-being. Through meditation, you cultivate the ability to quiet the mind and observe the world, and yourself, with greater clarity and presence. Breathwork goes a step further, enabling you to actively shift your energy, release emotional blockages, and access altered states of consciousness that might not be accessible through meditation alone.

Meditation and breathwork are more than just tools for relaxation, they're gateways to inner peace, clarity, and profound healing. These practices bridge the conscious and subconscious mind, helping you break through old patterns, release stuck emotions, and shift limiting beliefs. They're not about escaping the moment but grounding yourself fully in it, aligning your mind, body, and spirit with the natural flow of life. Whether it's a few quiet minutes or a deeper dedicated session, weaving these practices into your daily routine can transform how you feel, heal, and navigate your spiritual journey.

Mentors, Guides, & Experts

Iona Holloway

Iona Holloway, creator of the Soul app, offers transformative breathwork practices designed to help you release emotional blockages and reconnect with your inner power. Through her app, I've experienced the profound healing potential of breathwork, allowing me to clear away emotional clutter and find deeper clarity. Iona's approach is both intuitive and empowering, creating a space where breath becomes a tool for deep self-discovery and transformation. Her Soul app makes this practice accessible, offering guided breathwork sessions that have become an essential part of my personal growth journey.

bravething.co

NOTES

MAGICK

WHISPERED WORDS

Magick isn't confined to rituals under moonlit skies or spells whispered in the stillness. No, she's come to realize it lives in the cracks of her everyday life, waiting patiently to be noticed. She's learned to look for it, to invite it, to weave it into the mundane.

It starts in the morning, when sunlight spills through her window like liquid gold, painting her walls with the promise of a new day. She whispers a quiet blessing over her coffee as she stirs it, watching the steam curl upward like a message to the universe. With each sip, she sets her intention, gratitude, clarity, abundance. This, she thinks, is magick: simple, small acts imbued with meaning.

She feels the pull of water everywhere she goes. The way the morning dew glistens on her fingertips, cooling her skin as she gathers herbs for her tea. The rhythm of the river she passes on her walk, its gentle murmur filling her soul with serenity. Even washing her hands becomes a ritual of release, imagining the water carrying away her worries, leaving her palms open and ready to receive.

Her steps on the sidewalk feel like a rhythm, her breath syncing with the beat of her shoes against the ground. She notices the glint of sunlight on a puddle after the rain, the way it transforms into a mirror reflecting the sky above. She smiles, knowing this is the earth's quiet offering, a reminder of cycles and reflections, of how water connects her to everything it touches. She finds magick in the in-between moments. The feather that floats down onto her path, soft and white, as if placed there just for her. The way rain on her skin feels like a blessing, each drop carrying the whispers of clouds. The scent of lavender lingering on her skin from a ritual she performed the night before. The way a stranger's kind word feels like a spell of its own, lifting her spirits and turning her thoughts toward joy.

When she writes, her pen feels like a wand, casting spells with every stroke. Her words shape her reality, pulling dreams from the ether and planting them firmly in the soil of possibility. She lights a candle at her desk, its flame a tiny sun, a focus for her energy as she works. Even the act of tidying her space becomes magick, a cleansing ritual, clearing away what no longer serves her. And always, there's water, a sip of tea to ground her, a quick spritz of moon-charged mist to refresh her energy, a bowl of fresh *water placed on her altar to honor the element of flow.*

At the end of the day, she steps outside to greet the night sky. The stars twinkle like a thousand tiny spells cast long ago, each one a spark of the universe's infinite potential. She closes her eyes, feeling the energy of the day settle within her, grounding her, centering her. She speaks a quiet word of thanks, for the magick she's seen and the magick yet to come.

Magick with a K, she knows, isn't just about casting spells, it's about seeing the enchantment in life's smallest details. It's the way she chooses to walk through the world, eyes open to the wonders around her, heart open to the mysteries that lie just beyond. Every ripple in the water, every raindrop on her skin, every wave lapping against the shore reminds her: magick flows as freely as the tides, and she is its endless current.

Awakening the Magick Within: Embracing the Mystical

Magick, with a "K," is the art of intentional, conscious transformation. It's the practice of aligning your will and energy with the unseen forces of the universe to bring about change, healing, clarity, and power. Unlike the flashy illusions of pop culture, true magick is subtle, sacred, and deeply personal. It lives in ritual and rhythm, but also in the everyday, quietly asking you to notice, to listen, and to co-create with the energy that surrounds you.

To work magick is to become aware. It's not about control, but connection. When you practice magick, you're not commanding the universe; you're collaborating with it. You're stepping into the current and learning how to shape it with reverence and intention.

A Living Lineage: The History of Magick

Magick isn't new. It's ancient. It's the thread that's run through countless cultures and spiritual lineages for thousands of years. You'll find it in the sand-carved altars of Egypt, in the fires of the Celtic festivals, in the chants of the forest-dwelling shamans, and the spells whispered over cauldrons in village kitchens. It's been called many things, witchcraft, alchemy, mysticism, but at its core, it's always been about working with the forces we cannot see to shape the life we can.

As it evolved, magick branched into countless forms, ceremonial traditions, intuitive folk practices, elemental rites, and chaos systems, but its soul remained the same: a practice of intentional, energetic creation.

Paths of Magick

There is no one right way to practice magick. The path is yours to shape. Here are just a few:

- **Ceremonial Magick:** Structured, symbolic, and steeped in tradition, ceremonial magick is the sacred architecture of the spiritual world. It involves intricate rituals, invocations, sacred geometry, planetary timing, and tools like wands, robes, and ritual circles. Practitioners often work with divine beings, angels, or spiritual archetypes. This form of magick requires study and discipline, and it appeals to those who find power in sacred structure and timeless lineage.
- **Witchcraft:** Rooted in the earth and cycles of nature, witchcraft is intuitive, ancestral, and alive. It honors the divine in all things, stones, plants, seasons, and stars. Witches often work with lunar cycles, herbal

allies, deities, and the wheel of the year. Spellwork might include candle magick, kitchen rituals, knot spells, or divination. Witchcraft is a deeply personal path that blends ritual with daily life, making the mundane sacred and the sacred accessible.

- **Chaos Magick:** Chaos magick is the rebel of the magickal world. It strips away dogma and asks, "What works?" It treats belief as a tool rather than a truth, allowing practitioners to shape and shift symbols, rituals, and systems based on what feels effective in the moment. You might borrow from multiple traditions or make up your own sigils, affirmations, or paradigms. The only rule in chaos magick is that your intent is clear and your will is focused. It's raw, experimental, and liberating.

- **Folk Magick:** Practical and powerful, folk magick is the ancestral wisdom passed down through generations. It uses what's at hand, salt, eggshells, herbs, string, coins, and blends it with deep-rooted beliefs about protection, luck, healing, and home. You'll find folk magick in Appalachian granny traditions, Curanderismo, Hoodoo, Slavic household rites, and many more. It's often interwoven with cultural customs and spiritual practices. It's humble, direct, and rooted in relationship to land, lineage, and local spirits.

Each path is valid. Each is sacred. What matters most is that your practice feels aligned with your truth, your ancestry, and your personal sense of wonder and power.

The Elements: Foundations of Magickal Work

The elements, earth, air, fire, and water, are the building blocks of magick. When you work with them, you're not just using symbols. You're engaging with the soul of the natural world.

- **Earth** is grounding, stabilizing. It supports prosperity, physical health, and rooted intention.
- **Air** is clarity and communication. It stirs ideas, intuition, and truth.
- **Fire** is willpower, transformation, and passion. It fuels your courage and burns away stagnation.
- **Water** is emotion, intuition, and healing. It flows, it nurtures, and it connects.

Magick becomes powerful when you bring these forces into your rituals, your altars, and your everyday practices. Burn a candle for fire. Stir your tea with intention for water. Speak your affirmations into the wind. Sit barefoot on the earth and listen.

Making It Real: Daily Magick and Ritual

Magick doesn't require elaborate altars or ancient words (though those can be beautiful, too). It begins the moment you become intentional.

- **Create Sacred Space:** This could be a dedicated altar or just a windowsill with a candle and a crystal. Let it be a place where your energy feels anchored and seen.
- **Rituals and Spells:** A ritual can be as simple as lighting a candle and speaking your truth aloud. Spells are intentional acts, infused with emotion and clarity. Use herbs, water, oils, stones, breath, whatever feels resonant.
- **Work with the Moon:** The lunar cycle is a powerful guide. Set intentions during the New Moon. Manifest or release with the Full Moon. Waxing moons are for building. Waning moons are for clearing.
- **Keep a Magick Journal:** Document your rituals, your dreams, your results. Patterns will emerge. Insights will deepen. You'll begin to notice how powerful you truly are.
- **Enchant the Everyday:** Stir intention into your morning coffee, speak blessings into your bathwater, or trace sigils into your lotion before you rub it on your skin. Daily acts become sacred when you infuse them with purpose.
- **Connect with the Elements**: Choose one element each day to honor. Burn incense for air, light a match for fire, touch water to your skin, or carry a stone for earth. Let the element guide your focus and attune you to its energy.
- **Pull a Daily Card:** Draw a tarot or oracle card each morning. Let it be your guide, your reminder, or your mirror. Place it on your altar or carry it with you to anchor your awareness as the day unfolds.

Why Magick Matters

Magick isn't just about making things happen. It's about remembering that you are not powerless. It's about reclaiming agency in a world that so often tells us to stay small. When you practice magick, you shift from reactive to intentional. From fragmented to whole. From watching your life unfold to shaping it with care.

Magick teaches you to be in relationship with the land, the sky, your ancestors, your body, your breath. It reminds you that everything is alive, everything is energy, and everything can be honored.

And above all, it reminds you that the sacred isn't somewhere far away. It's here. In your tea, your breath, your tears, your laughter. In your messy desk and your moonlit prayers. In your choice to bless your day before it begins. This is magick, too.

You are the spell. You are the altar. You are the living, breathing ritual. So go ahead. Stir your coffee with a wish. Light a candle and speak your truth. Clean your home with intention. Place water on your altar and speak to the moon. This is your power. This is your practice. This is your magick.

Mentors, Guides, and Experts

Tamed Wild

Tamed Wild has been a beautiful source of magick and inspiration in my spiritual practice. Their offerings, from ritual tools to guides on ancient wisdom, have helped me reconnect with the power of everyday magick. Through their website, I've found everything I need to create meaningful rituals, align with lunar cycles, and deepen my connection to the elements. Tamed Wild blends modern accessibility with ancient practices, making it easy to incorporate magick into daily life. Whether it's a ritual kit or a piece of sacred jewelry, every item feels intentional and alive with energy, helping me keep my practice vibrant and grounded in ancient wisdom.

tamedwild.com

Magic of I

Magic of I has been an essential part of my practice, especially through their beautifully crafted journals and astrological calendars. Their tools not only keep me organized but also align me with the cosmic rhythms of the universe. The level of detail in their astrological calendars has helped me track the phases of the moon, planetary movements, and how these energies influence my daily life. Their journals provide a space for reflection and intention-setting, making my connection to the stars and my inner world even deeper. With Magic of I, each day feels infused with meaning, helping me live more in sync with the natural and cosmic cycles.

magicofi.com

NOTES

GROUNDING & CENTERING

Whispered Words

One step into the forest, and the shift begins. The air feels different here, cooler, quieter, alive with an energy that hums beneath her feet. Worries that once pressed against her chest soften, like mist dissolving in sunlight. She feels the connection start to rise, like the steady flow of a river embracing her, carrying her back to herself.

The trees speak to her in whispers, their voices rustling through the leaves, their roots stretching toward her in welcome. Each step she takes brings her closer to her center, closer to the knowing that resides deep within, the place that belongs to her and her alone.

She pauses to breathe, to feel. The forest wraps itself around her, a sanctuary of green and gold. Here, she is not separate but part of the whole: one with the trees that stretch toward the heavens, one with the water that carves its path through the earth, one with the creatures that rustle unseen in the underbrush.

Grounded once more, she feels her breath deepen, her heartbeat steady. Her fingers brush against the rough bark of an ancient oak, the grooves and ridges telling stories older than she can imagine. She raises her face to the canopy above, where light filters through in soft beams, warming her skin and filling her spirit.

Her hands press into the moss, soft and alive beneath her touch, as if the earth itself is breathing with her. The rhythm of the forest slows her, centers her. She listens, not just to the sounds of nature, but to the whispers of her own soul.

Breathing.
Listening.
Connecting.
Knowing.
Slowing.

In this moment, she is whole. In this space, she is alive again, rooted to the earth, cradled by the forest, and centered in her own light.

The Power of Grounding and Centering

Grounding and centering is the art of reconnecting with yourself and the earth, creating a sense of inner balance and stability in a fast-paced world. It's about slowing down, stepping outside into nature, and feeling the ground beneath you, whether it's bare feet on the grass, the cool earth beneath your palms, or the breeze that reminds you to breathe deeply.

Grounding and centering are like plugging into the Earth's outlet and getting back to you. Imagine you're a tree, and those roots need to dig into the soil to find stability, nourishment, and connection. That's grounding. It's about anchoring your energy, letting go of the mental noise, and allowing the Earth's stability to balance you out. Whether it's touching the ground, breathing deeply, or visualizing roots growing from your feet, grounding brings you back to a place where you can feel calm, safe, and steady, even when life gets chaotic.

Centering, on the other hand, is like focusing on the still point within you, a place that is uniquely yours, where your power and inner wisdom reside. It's about finding your balance in the storm, like a compass needle aligning with true north. When you center yourself, you're gathering all your scattered thoughts and emotions back into that core space. It's the feeling of being in tune with your own energy, knowing that no matter what's swirling around you, you are whole, solid, and present.

Together, grounding and centering are how you come home to yourself, ready to face the world with clarity and purpose.

Grounding in Nature

Nature is one of the most powerful tools for grounding and centering yourself. The earth carries a stabilizing energy, and by consciously connecting with it, you align yourself with its steady rhythm. When life feels chaotic, the simple act of walking barefoot on the earth, hugging a tree, or sitting by a river can help clear mental fog, reduce anxiety, and bring you back into the present moment. Grounding is all about reconnecting to the physical world, the here and now.

This practice is as simple as it sounds. Go outside and take off your shoes. Feel the dirt, the grass, the rocks under your feet, and let your body absorb the earth's natural energy. When you ground yourself in nature, you're not just physically reconnecting; you're energetically releasing stress, negative thoughts, and anything that pulls you out of alignment.

Grounding When You Can't Get to Nature

Not everyone has access to a forest trail or riverside view, but grounding and centering are still fully within reach, no matter where you are. Your home, office, or even a quiet moment on public transit can become a sacred space with a little intention.

Start with breath. Wherever you are, take a few slow, deep breaths. Feel the weight of your body in your chair or your feet on the floor. Close your eyes and imagine roots growing from your feet, extending deep into the earth. Even a brief moment of visualization can shift your energy.

You can also use tactile tools. Keep grounding stones like Black Tourmaline or Hematite nearby. Touch something solid, your desk, a wall, a textured fabric, and use that connection as a reminder of your presence in the physical world. Aromatherapy can also help; grounding essential oils like vetiver, cedarwood, or patchouli offer instant earthiness and calm.

Engage your senses: put on calming music, drink warm tea, or run your hands under cool water with intention. Each of these actions brings you back into your body and the moment, no forest required.

Centering Your Energy

While grounding connects you to the earth, centering brings you back to your core. It's about focusing inward, finding that still point within where you can access clarity and calm amidst the noise of everyday life. When you feel scattered, overwhelmed, or anxious, centering helps you gather your energy, reclaim your focus, and restore balance.

There are several ways to center yourself. A simple method is through mindful breathing, take deep, intentional breaths and imagine your energy pooling in your center, often felt in the solar plexus or heart space. Visualization is another powerful tool: picture a golden light or a peaceful scene in your mind's eye and let it anchor you back to your core.

The Power of Slowing Down

In a world that's constantly demanding speed and productivity, one of the most radical things you can do is slow down. Grounding and centering remind us that we are not machines; we are beings in a natural rhythm, and sometimes that rhythm needs a pause. Take the time to step outside, breathe deeply, and simply be. When you slow down and root yourself in the present moment, you create space for healing, clarity, and the inner peace you crave.

Creating Rituals for Grounding and Centering

Integrating grounding and centering into your daily practice doesn't have to be complicated. You can create small rituals that help anchor you throughout the day, especially when life feels hectic. Whether it's a morning walk in nature, a five-minute breathing exercise before bed, or simply touching the earth with intention, these rituals serve as a reminder that you are always connected to the energy around and within you.

Crystals like Black Tourmaline, Hematite, and Smoky Quartz are also powerful tools for grounding. Keep them close, meditate with them, or carry them in your pocket as a reminder to stay rooted in your body and the present moment. For centering, crystals like Amethyst or Clear Quartz can help align your energy and bring you back to your inner balance.

Grounding and Centering in a Modern World

We live in a fast-paced, tech-heavy world that can often pull us away from our natural state of balance. Grounding and centering practices act as the antidote to this disconnection. When you take the time to reconnect with the earth, slow down, and focus inward, you remind yourself of what it means to be fully present and embodied. You clear away the mental clutter, emotional overload, and stress, and step back into your own power.

Grounding and centering aren't just tools for when you're feeling lost or overwhelmed; they are daily practices that can keep you aligned with your true self, helping you navigate life with more grace, peace, and intention.

Imagine finding yourself in a quiet forest, the trees gently swaying, or sitting by a river, the sound of water lapping at the shore. Or maybe you are in your apartment, lighting a candle and placing your hands over your heart. Maybe it's standing barefoot on your balcony, or closing your eyes on the subway and focusing on your breath. These moments, whether surrounded by nature or carved out of everyday environments, are powerful reminders of the stillness and balance that always exist beneath the surface of life's chaos. In those spaces, you can breathe deeply, let go, and simply be.

Whether it's the hush of the woods, the hum of the city, or the quiet between tasks, allow yourself to reconnect with that grounded, centered place inside. These moments are not luxuries; they are essential pauses that restore your balance and remind you of the simple, powerful energy that sustains you. Make space for this in your life; you deserve it.

Mentors, Guides, and Experts

Katherine Genet

Katherine Genet, author of Ground and Centre, has a way of weaving spirituality into everyday life in a way that feels grounding, practical, and deeply connected to nature. Her book resonated with me on such a profound level, offering insights into how we can root ourselves in the earth while simultaneously opening up to the vast expanse of spiritual energy around us. Genet's writing encourages you to slow down, find stillness, and reconnect with both your inner world and the natural world. Ground and Centre has become one of my go-to reads when I need to reset, re-center, and find my footing in both life and my spiritual practice.

katherinegenet.online

NOTES

CRYSTALS

WHISPERED WORDS

They call to her, each one with a voice as unique as its shimmer. Walking into the shop, she feels their energy before she sees them, a gentle hum that rises as she draws closer. The crystals sit quietly, yet their presence fills the room. She doesn't pick them; they pick her, their pull undeniable, their purpose clear.

Her hands hover over the clusters of amethyst, the smooth tumble of rose quartz, the sharp points of clear quartz. She waits, listening not with her ears but with her spirit, for the subtle shift in energy, the way one stone seems to glow just for her. When she picks it up, there's a spark, a resonance. She smiles, knowing this is the one.

Each crystal is more than a stone; it's a keeper of energy, a partner in her journey. They rest on her altar, in her pocket, on her windowsill, catching the light and amplifying her intentions. The cool weight of a piece of smoky quartz in her hand grounds her when the world feels too heavy. A small carnelian sits at her desk, its warmth fueling her creativity. And by her bedside, an amethyst point keeps her dreams clear and calm.

She cleanses them with care, holding them under running water or letting them bathe in the glow of the full moon. She whispers gratitude as she works, knowing these crystals are more than tools, they are allies, holding her intentions, magnifying her energy, and helping her move through life with clarity and purpose.

When she meditates, they guide her deeper. A clear quartz in her palm feels like a key, unlocking a door to a higher plane of understanding. Placing a piece of labradorite on her third eye, she feels her intuition sharpen, her thoughts expanding into realms she couldn't access before. It's as if the stones themselves are maps, showing her the way back to herself. Their presence is constant, whether she's crafting a ritual or simply carrying one in her pocket as a quiet companion. They remind her to be intentional, to align her energy with her desires. Each crystal carries a lesson, a message: trust in the process, stay grounded, shine brightly, embrace transformation.

To her, crystals are more than beautiful treasures of the earth. They are fragments of the universe, ancient and wise, each one holding a spark *of the cosmos. When she holds them, she feels connected to something greater, to the earth, to the stars, to herself.*

And so, she listens to their call, letting their energy guide her, trusting that these shimmering stones will always lead her to exactly where she needs to be.

Sacred Stones: Harnessing the Energy of Crystals

This chapter might be one of my favorites to write. I have had a love affair with crystals for my entire life. I wouldn't say I understood their power or how to use them, but there was just something about crystals or even rocks and shells that drew me to them. I might have a slight obsession. Have you ever picked up a stone and it feels as if it is humming or pulsing in your hand. Like it really feels alive, well spoiler alert…. They are!

Crystals contain energy just like any other living thing. They have properties that can help you along your life's journeys, if you are open to it and are willing to work with them. In 2018, I went on my first crystal dig and from that moment on, I knew it was more than just rocks in the dirt. More than just things collecting dust on a shelf, if you allow them to be and allow them to work with you in your life.

Crystals are like ancient whispers from the earth, humming with an energy that speaks to those who listen. Their vibrations carry wisdom and healing properties that have been shaped over millennia. When you hold a crystal, you're connecting with the pulse of the universe itself.

To truly tap into their power, it's about creating a sacred relationship. Start by attuning to their energy, hold them in meditation, place them on your altar, or carry them close. Each stone has its own purpose. For example, Clear Quartz is a master healer, amplifying the intentions you set, while Black Tourmaline offers grounding protection from negativity.

In your practice, work intuitively with them. Sit with your crystal in silence and let it speak to you, feel its vibrations sync with yours. For protection, place Amethyst by your bedside to create a spiritual shield in your sleep, or use Citrine for manifesting abundance by placing it in the wealth corner of your home.

Crystals can even be used in moon rituals, allowing them to bask in lunar energy overnight to recharge their power. Feel their energy, respect their ancient nature, and, most importantly, open your heart to their subtle magick. It's not about "using" them; it's about partnering with them as spiritual allies on your path.

When you fully invite them into your life, crystals don't just sit on a shelf, they become living, breathing companions, here to guide, heal, and elevate your energy. The more you open yourself to their wisdom, the more you'll realize they're not just stones; they are the earth's heartbeat, pulsing through your journey.

Connecting with crystals begins with intention and respect. To truly build a relationship, start by holding your crystal in your hands, close your eyes, and breathe deeply. Feel its energy and let it harmonize with your own. Set your intentions clearly, whether it's for healing, protection, or manifesting, and allow the crystal to amplify that energy.

Caring for your crystals is just as important. Cleanse them regularly by placing them in sunlight, moonlight, or using smoke to clear away absorbed energies. Keep them charged and attuned, and they'll serve as powerful allies on your spiritual journey. Always treat them with reverence, as they're not mere objects but partners in your journey of growth and healing.

It's important to remember that working with them is a deeply personal journey. Whether you're using them for healing, meditation, or manifesting, the key is to trust your intuition and connect with their energy. As you build this relationship, crystals become more than just tools; they are companions, guiding you toward deeper self-awareness and spiritual growth. Their energy is ancient and wise, and when you invite them into your life, they open doors to transformation in ways both subtle and profound.

Mentors, Guides, and Experts

Rachel Hancock

The Ultimate Guide to Crystals by Rachel Hancock is a comprehensive resource for those interested in the healing energy of crystals and stones. This guide offers detailed profiles of 100 crystals, covering their physical properties, chakra associations, and healing benefits. It also provides insights into integrating crystals into practices like feng shui, meditation, and reiki. Rachel Hancock, a Certified Advanced Crystal Practitioner and Reiki Master, brings her expertise to this work, making it accessible for both beginners and seasoned practitioners. For those looking to deepen their understanding of crystal healing, The Ultimate Guide to Crystals serves as a valuable tool, offering practical advice and comprehensive information to support personal growth and well-being.

lovingthyselfrocks.com

NOTES

CONCLUSION

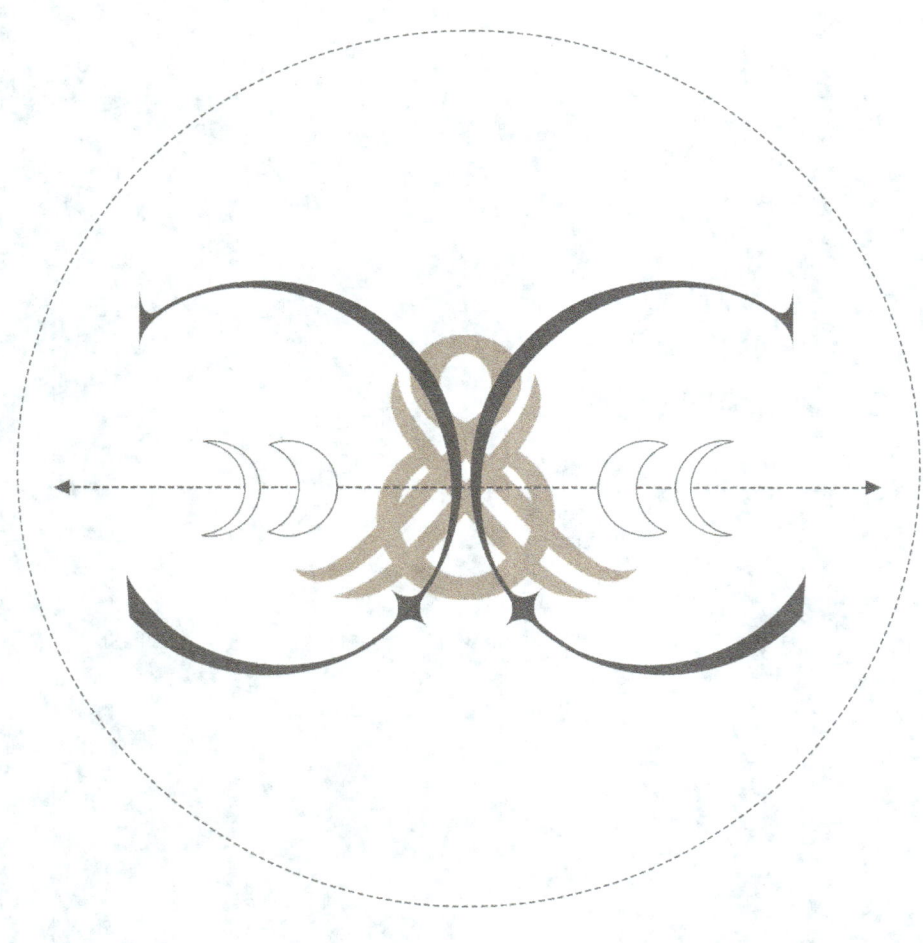

Conclusion: A Life Full of Magick and Meaning

This book has been a journey, starting with clarity, weaving through the vast and mystical realms of metaphysical practices, and ending with the grounding beauty of crystals. Each chapter has been a spotlight, shining on the wisdom, guides, and mentors who have shaped my path and inspired me to share this journey with you. From spirit guides and ancestors to astrology, shamanism, meditation, and magick, this book offers an introduction to practices that have brought profound transformation to my life.

I want to take a moment to thank the incredible mentors, guides, and experts who have illuminated my path and whose wisdom has shaped the pages of this book. From those who introduced me to new practices and ideas, to those who offered guidance during pivotal moments in my journey, your influence has been immeasurable. Your light has not only inspired me but also allowed me to share these insights with others. This book is as much a reflection of your wisdom as it is my journey. Thank you for being the guiding stars that continue to shine so brightly.

Through the lens of my own experiences, I've hoped to show how accessible and life-changing these tools can be. Whether you're grounding yourself in nature, working with crystals, or connecting with your inner wisdom, there's a universal truth: the journey begins within.
Clarity and Crystals isn't just a book; it's a doorway. It's a place to explore, experiment, and expand your spiritual practice. My goal has always been to demystify these practices, making them approachable while honoring their depth and ancient roots.

This journey doesn't end here, it continues to evolve, and you can follow along at Clarity and Crystals, where I share more about my experiences, insights, and the guides who inspire me. The website is an extension of this book, a space to deepen your understanding, discover new practices, and connect with a community of like-minded souls.

For me, this journey has been about learning to trust myself, to find the magick in the everyday, and to embrace the infinite possibilities the metaphysical offers. As you turn the final page, know that your journey is just beginning. From clarity to crystals, and everything in between, I hope you carry the light of this exploration into your own life, creating magick, healing, and connection wherever you go.

Thank you for letting me share my journey with you. Now, it's your turn to let the spotlight shine on your own path. Remember, this is just the beginning. The magick doesn't stop when you close the book.

Head over to clarityandcrystals.com for more ways to explore, expand, and stay connected.

~ Angie

www.ingramcontent.com/pod-product-compliance
Lightning Source LLC
Chambersburg PA
CBHW070344130626
46556CB00007B/3020